SHINE!

Now is the time for you to shine!
Embrace who you are meant to be.
The world needs your light!

SONJA SCHWEIZER

Copyright 2022 © Sonja Schweizer

All Rights Reserved. No part of this book may be reproduced in any manner whatsoever, or stored in any information storage system, or transmitted in any form or by any means, electronic, mechanical, photocopying, recording, or otherwise, without the prior written consent of the publisher, except in the case of brief quotations with proper reference, embodied in articles and reviews.

ISBN: 978-0-6452371-5-3

Thank you

I'm utterly filled with gratitude.

A huge thank you and all my love to Kurt, my hubby, who means the world to me.

To ALL the people who supported me with their expertise and hearts while writing this book, and to all my friends and mentors who have always believed in me.

To all the people who have shared a connection or an adventure with me, or both!

To all the people who expanded my universe.

And thank you to you, dear reader, for your curiosity and for allowing me to touch your heart.

What you can expect from reading and working with this book and answering the questions.

A lot- be curious! About yourself, about others, about the world.

Some stories you will relate to, you will know exactly what the author is talking about because you have experienced fear, anxiety, claustrophobia, and self-doubts in your own life or have witnessed this in the life of your loved ones.

Some stories may feel comfortable because you've been through it and have come out victorious on the other side.

In this you will experience appreciation towards yourself for all that you have already accomplished.

You will be invited to look at things and situations from another perspective.

You will become aware of the infinite possibilities you may choose from in this life.

You will be stimulated and invited to connect to your dreams, the clear and the hidden ones, so that you can create your Heart List.

What matters most to you will become clear.

You will gain awareness about what excites you, where you need to adapt to get what you really want.

You will start to feel more energized as you read each week's story, and as you get more involved in the stories, as you live each story alongside the protagonist, you will feel fresh light being shone onto your dreams- not only through the stories of the protagonist, but with yours too.

Allow yourself to experience whatever your heart is longing for. Open yourself up to your heart and what it is trying to tell you. Listen for its voice- you will know it when you hear it.

While reading this book you will empower yourself to take responsibility for your own happiness, and the exciting and refreshing moments that bring you inner peace.

FOREWORD

Sometimes, very rarely, we come across a moment, a person or an experience, that takes our breath away. These moments, these people, these experiences stay imprinted in our memory forever. When we think of them, we are filled with a sense of joy and nostalgia, and yet we can no longer touch the physical part of what we once encountered. Sonja's book is one of those moments, one of those experiences... Sonja is one of those people.

I had the pleasure of meeting Sonja before she embarked on her magical journey of writing this book. When she spoke, I found that the world made sense. Her absolute joy for life and everything in it inspired me to look a little deeper, feel a little more, and linger a little longer. She had so much life to share with me and so much that she could teach me, and yet I was the one coaching her. You see, Sonja had discovered something that only a few people I know have found. She had discovered herself. And in that, she had found the true purpose of life – joy.

While many books claim to inspire their readers to 'go out there and find yourself', there are only a select few that really do light that fire under us. With droves of life coaches and consultants entering – and already in – the market of self-development, it often feels as if the story is unchanged. Their natural high from life is often unattainable by millions, and yet we continue to read their books and follow their courses, hoping that one day we too will leap out of bed with a changed perspective of our lives, ready to continue for the rest of our days with only joy, forgiveness, and purpose. But it is clear from the current state of our world that this is not the case. It would be expected that with so much self-development on the go, we would be the perfect society. Surely by now, everyone has found themselves, given to those less fortunate, and created balance in their lives and within the Universe? Of course, that is not the case. And we continue to watch the world go by as broken as it has ever been with its people seeking happiness, if only for a minute and even if it is illusory and manufactured.

This book is different. Not because it will answer all your questions and make you change your perspective overnight, but because while you read it you will discover, through the personal stories that Sonja shares, page by page, day by day, that you dear reader *are* the story. Sonja will take you on a glittering, often hysterically funny journey of life, of moments that took her breath away, moments that made her notice that She is… so much more than enough. Experiences that made her realise that She always has been, and always will be the story of life. What a wonderful gift Sonja gives to the world! The gift that in each and every one of us is strength, love, joy, forgiveness, and peace. The gift to rediscover, that these vital parts of ourselves – which we so desperately seek externally – have always been there, inside of us…

This book is a reminder of who we are, not an instruction manual of how we should be, and what we need to do or what we need to become to be happy. To find joy, we simply need to look in the mirror and *love* what we see. The bombardment of thoughts, questions and doubt we run through our minds on a daily basis, are distractions.

They are not what we are, but rather what we are not. To clear the mind, to silence the chatter and see Her for who She is in all her proud and golden glory, is pure joy.

The joy of being alive – it permeates every page of this book. She will remind you of the moments, people, and experiences that have brought you joy. She will remind you that there are many, if not thousands, of little joys every day. She will take you there with every sight, sound and smell. She will make you question why you are no longer noticing these little joys. She will bring you home. She will help you shine. If you are reading this, then you are already on your way to where you belong. Don't stop now.

Dr. Samantha Worthington (MBA)
Global Coach and Mentor

Do you remember the time of in-between? Standing between the ages, not a teenager anymore but still not really belonging to the world of adults. Exploring your newfound freedom by travelling, leaving what you know to visit foreign countries, letting go of security and being taken care of to step into adventure. She's chosen to be an au pair, with responsibility but flexibility. She's not able to speak in her mother tongue while working; instead, she stumbles through a foreign language. During this in-between season of her life, this is what is required of her. New skills must quickly be developed. Sometimes, how things show up is not how we expected them to.

ENGLAND PART 1 - IN-BETWEEN

She leaves her home country to go to England; a girl, becoming a woman. She will be on her own for the first time, and even more exciting, it will be her first flight- she's never flown before. It's a short trip but it's all so unfamiliar to her. Her thoughts whirl around, her stomach uneasy.

She is proud of herself and her courage- considering that she does not know what to expect and what challenges are waiting for her. As an au pair, she will often find herself in situations she has never experienced before. Growing up in a protected environment, being the only child, not tremendously spoiled but still getting all the attention a child with no siblings gets, life will now be a totally different story! In a way, this year will be like an initiation for her.

She arrives safely in London after a bumpy flight. She gets picked up by her new family with whom she will spend the next year. She sits on the backseat of the car between the two prepubescent and pubescent eleven- and thirteen-year-old boys, the ones she has to look after while their parents, both full-time entrepreneurs, are at work. The first conversation is about their guinea pigs, but she has real difficulty in understanding even one word. It's too late for her to change her mind. Of course, she knew a huge challenge lay ahead of her if she chose to stay in a country where they speak a different language- English, in this case, which happened to be her weakest subject at school. Why had she chosen to expose herself like this? Well, to learn a foreign language they say it makes sense to live in the country where they speak it. It is already clear that English is the language which most people in the world are going to have to learn in order to communicate and do business with each other.

Besides doing the household chores, she tries to cook for them, but it's clearly more trying than succeeding! Especially because she only learned basic cooking skills in school. But day by day she gets better at it; she refuses to give up, and slowly gets herself more organized. The boys have to wear a school uniform, and she is in charge of making sure that everything is clean and in its place. Suddenly she sees herself between the two boys, not much older, but already having to take responsibility for them, trying to gain some authority and be accepted. Sometimes she feels alone and homesick; it's difficult to find someone to talk to in her mother tongue. Phone calls home cost a lot of money; the internet doesn't exist yet.

Attending her weekly English class has become the highlight of her week, allowing her to meet new people and take a break from just being a maid! It's always a treat to get together with the other au pairs, more or less the same age as her. She enjoys meeting them at the English teacher's private home, an English cottage in the countryside, sitting at her long kitchen table, sipping on a cup of English tea and eating a ginger cookie while trying to have a conversation in English with her teacher and the other students. Her teacher not only teaches her the language, but also shares valuable knowledge about what makes England so special- the history, the society, and, of course, the royalty. Her teaching is a comforting haven for all the au pairs, a place to go to if something is bothering them. She knows she has to work hard to get ready to take the Oxford First Certificate and pass it. She sees herself as a phoenix rising from the ashes.

Before her first year is even over, her host family cancels her contract. The reason for their decision is that they want a more permanent au pair. They don't want to end up without any help when the time comes for her to leave.

Her new family is set to receive her as a part of their family as soon as she is ready. If she had known the situation beforehand, perhaps she would have made different decisions- chosen this family from the start. But she has always been the type of person who feels responsible for the wellbeing of everyone around her. She's only able to focus on herself when she knows that everyone around her is happy. With the new family, everything gets much better: more warmth, more family life, four kids, three dogs, more conversations, she is more integrated and more appreciated. She takes walks with the youngest, a two-year-old girl, through the garden, having a chat, surveying the garden and hearing the young girl say things to her like, *Mind the dog pooh*!

It's so refreshing. She feels alive. The four children become like her siblings: she's only two or three years older than the eldest two. It's a whole new world for her. She even gets used to the dogs, feeding them and giving them attention, and because of this very intimate and personal act, becoming their best friend.

Being in the kitchen with her young landlady, preparing a delicious meal, is also a wonderful experience for her. It's like being in a family. She feels privileged to be in this family, finally understanding the power of being open to others, leading with your heart, being spontaneous, and being open to unexpected situations. She gets invited to join relaxing parties at their poolside. To be a part of this colorful life is more than she could have wished for. She learns this and so much more from this wonderful, loving, and caring family. In the end, everything comes together in a great potpourri example of how different life can be if you are willing to try new things.

QUESTIONS

- Do you remember a situation of initiation in your adolescence?
- When did you feel clearly, for the first time, your own power and strength?
- What gave you comfort in your earlier years?
- Have you ever confronted a weakness of yours, a skill which was underdeveloped? What was it?
- What were the steps you took to improve it?
- Is there a specific uncertainty, a deficiency, something you have tried to hide but now feel and know that it's time to reveal it and set it free?
- If so, what will be your concrete and realistic action steps from start to finish to set this secret free?

If we are willing to be brave, learning new skills can be a challenge as well as a great opportunity to expand the universe we live in. I often ask myself, what's the worst that can happen? What will happen if I fail? Well, the world will surely keep turning and I will still be lovable, I will still be enough. I think the more important question to ask yourself is: What do I risk by *not* trying?

ENGLAND PART 2 - FIRST TIME ON HER OWN

She is now eighteen and finally learning to drive. She is already challenging herself; she knows that driving in England is done on the left-hand side of the road, not like other countries in Europe where one drives on the right. If she pictures herself driving through all the different countries around the world, she can see that she will eventually get used to the left-hand-side traffic. Everything in life has a point of view, and often our own points of view are only half of the picture. There are left- and right-hand sides to everything. If she wants to see the world, she is going to have to learn to adapt to both.

She can barely understand the accent of her very strict Scottish driving test expert. He tells her that the student who took the test before her failed. Already nervous, this unsettling news is not the start she wished to have. *Take a deep breath*, she says to herself, and off she drives. *You can trust yourself.* You passed! Yes, that's what she was hoping to hear. Relieved, and with a big smile on her face, she exits the car and feels as though she could fly. She is elated.

Even though she is now legally allowed to drive a car, she asks a good friend if she may borrow her bicycle to travel around with, to see some parts of the south of England. She is blown away by her friend's generosity – she just bought a new bicycle, and she may borrow it for her road trip. What an adventure! First, she packs the side bags of her new horse-powered two-wheel vehicle with what she will need for her trip. The start of the trip is easy; she gets on the train which takes her directly into the city of London. From there she must ride her bike through the bustling city streets, crossing the Piccadilly Circus junction, trying to stay on the bike while swerving to miss the iconic black cabs! After surviving the mayhem that is London traffic, she hops onto another train that takes her further south. English weather is known for its unfriendliness: rain, fog, and wind. Dark, melancholic skies. She starts getting in touch with this uncomfortable companion. When she rides downhill, she must use the pedals if she plans to stand a chance against the strong wind that threatens from every direction to throw her off course, to hamper her cycling experience. At times, when the power of nature overwhelms her, she gets off her bicycle and pushes it. No matter the weather or the challenges it poses, she feels powerful overcoming the voice within her telling her that she should be scared, that she shouldn't be enjoying herself in these conditions. She doesn't give up. She is open enough to receive. She meets kind people along the way and appreciates the scenery of this rugged terrain and the fields surrounded by stone walls. There are flocks of sheep dining on luscious green grass as far as the eye can see. She stays at youth hostels where she cooks small meals for herself, trying new foods, enjoying the communal experience filled with all sorts of conversations with other bikers or hikers. She loves the convenience of having a comfortable, safe place to sleep and recharge her batteries, ready for the next day's muscle-exerting bike workout. One particular youth hostel is right on the cliffs. When she lies in bed at night, trying to fall asleep, she hears how intensively the waves splash against the rocks and the cliff. It's quite unnerving, almost frightening to hear this spectacle so close to where she's sleeping. But why not experience this just once? She feels so fortunate to be able to explore such a world, so new to her. There are red telephone boxes in the town. She gets her coins ready to make a short call home. But the Universe steps in and a miracle happens! The connection doesn't cut out when her money is finished – she doesn't have to use any more coins to stay on the call, instead she can go on talking for as long as she wishes. What a great gift. Afterwards, she hits the road again.

She is almost at her next destination when there's a small problem with her bike. A flat wheel is a minor hiccup. She leaves it at a bike shop in a small village which is close to the next hostel she'll be staying in. She gets on a bus which takes her to her next stay. It's a cozy youth hostel at the headland of the island, where, from above, she can look down and ahead onto the rough sea. She is completely captivated by being that far out in nature. It's so archaic, remote, and untamed.

In the morning, another guest's car is having trouble starting. Her new skill as a driver is tested as she must sit in the driver's seat and subtly play with the gas and the clutch to get the engine turning while the others push the car downhill. It's a perfect team effort. Eureka!

She can hear the motor buzzing; the mission has been successfully accomplished. This is her first experience being a real driver after having passed her driving test. She had to overcome her self-doubt in that moment and jump into action. What a good start to the next part of her journey; a good omen.

Later in the day, she decides to walk back to the village to collect her newly repaired bicycle. While she walks along the only street there is, the wild of her natural surroundings flanking her sides, suddenly a thick fog creeps in from all four compass points. She can hardly see where she's going. There is a faint outline of something in the field next to her. At first, she doesn't trust her eyes when she sees a stone circle emerge. It's so mystical, almost eerie. It's surreal and confusing to be unexpectedly in contact with another era, another epoch. She doesn't feel very comfortable being there, especially with next to no visibility. She realizes she will have to hitchhike. There is a first time for everything! Luckily it doesn't take long for a car to stop. The woman offering her a lift explains that she usually never picks up people she doesn't know. Not having to be on their own in this otherworldly weather, they welcome each other's company and expand their mindsets just by talking to each other. What a great opportunity for the two of them to surrender themselves to forces greater than their understanding.

QUESTIONS

- What are some of the adventures you experienced during your adolescence?
- What happened on each occasion?
- What kind of skills did you develop through each experience, or realize you already had within you?
- What did you learn from every adventure?
- Which of those skills have you forgotten about, and would love to welcome back into your life now as an adult?
- Which ones are you going to invite into your life again?

What do you like to explore when you arrive at a new destination? Have you ever felt exposed and vulnerable in a different culture, where your look, skin color, or your whole being didn't really fit in? Did you stand out everywhere you went?

JAPAN HONEYMOON PART 1

She and her hubby love Chinese food and Japanese culture. That's why they decide to visit Japan. Perhaps it's more about experiencing an exotic world, a world they only know from books and movies. She is fascinated with those blooming cherry trees with their beguiling soft pink blossoms. Unfortunately, she has to sacrifice seeing them on this trip, because they agreed to visit Japan right after their wedding in fall. Yes, sometimes life doesn't present the gifts she wishes for at the exact moment she hopes for them. But what she didn't know was that she would get the opportunity to see the enchanting soft pink creations twenty years later while on their trip to Stockholm, walking out of a shopping mall, totally surprised by the beauty in a park right in front of her. A whole cosmos of trees, and all in full bloom, and she, right in the middle of it, engulfed by the intense sweet scent. What bliss.

They arrive at Tokyo airport. Her new husband has a three-day beard, and she has dyed her hair burgundy red. They haven't considered that this is exotic for the Japanese, and not the other way around. People stare and wave at them everywhere they go. They feel exposed, as if they are in full view of the entire Japanese population. Even while walking in a park, enjoying nature and the wonderful, sophisticated scenery, they are not on their own. Pupils dressed in their school uniforms approach her excitedly to ask if they can take a photo with her. She finds herself surrounded by giggling girls, all trying to stand as close as possible to her. She gets a glimpse of how celebrities must feel, wishing to be left alone or to go unnoticed. Or people who have a different skin color to that of the majority. One of the reasons to travel to other countries is to immerse yourself in unfamiliar cultures: their way of living, their food, their rituals, their nature, and their cultural expressions, in music, dancing, acting, travelling. Wherever she goes, she loves to visit the department stores, to see what the locals buy and enjoy. When they get out of the elevator on the top floor, they are surprised to find themselves in a bonsai and flower exhibition. They are amused when someone asks them if they are bonsai students, especially when they don't know anything about making an art piece out of flowers or meticulously arranging and pruning these miniature trees. They move around, taking in every detail of every piece of natural art. For the first time on their trip they see, in all her beauty, a Japanese woman wearing a traditional kimono. She presents herself in a quiet but confident manner. It is very impressive.

QUESTIONS

- How do you like to present yourself?
- Can you reach the point where you are just the observer in a situation and be present in what is going on around you?
- By not only scratching the surface, what hobby would you like to dive deeper into?
- In what ways or situations do you feel exposed? What is your solution if you don't feel comfortable?
- Where do you feel you are exotic?
- Where do you like to be seen and recognized? For what do you like to be acknowledged and praised?
- Would you like to grow even more into having an interest and openness in understanding the importance and meaning of things and situations that mean a lot to others but that you might not know much about? Where and what specifically?

Connection and communication are influenced by culture, especially how they are used to interact with others in daily life. What are the values of certain countries? With media, more so now than ever, this can get mixed up and confusing.

JAPAN HONEYMOON PART 2

She realizes that different cultures have different approaches to hospitality and communication. Being in Tokyo and asking someone for directions can become quite tricky. The Japanese are very polite and do not find it easy to say no and would rather give an answer which isn't helpful or is misleading.

She and her hubby quickly learn that the Japanese never truly say no, or instead, say it without saying it. The objective is to maintain harmony in every situation by not expressing themselves too directly to avoid offending someone. As is the case in many Asian countries, direct refusal is regarded as socially unacceptable.

In the end, they manage to find a way to take the correct train up to the mountains of Japan to an old traditional village. She loves to make herself comfortable in these sorts of scenarios. She sits and lets the scenery of a totally different Japan, with all its hills that pass by her window, open her up to enjoying this experience to the fullest. They stay at a Ryokan, a traditional guesthouse. People often visit Ryokans with the aim of relaxing in a peaceful and comfortable atmosphere. Ryokans focus on creating beautiful gardens, baths, and other common areas for their guests to enjoy.

One of the most popular things to do at a Ryokan is indulge in a hot bath. She and her hubby put on the Yukata, a traditional cotton garment, similar in style to a Kimono, only lighter and far more casual. Yukata can be worn as a bathrobe or loungewear, or even as pajamas. They head off together, but she steps alone into the bathing area for women. It is separated into two sections; the actual bathing area, and a section to wash the body. Luckily, she had already read up about the proper procedure of taking a bath at a Ryokan. She is on her own, so there is no one to mind how she does things.

Several wooden buckets are placed in a separate area of the room. First, she uses the soap to cleanse her body and then she fills the wooden buckets to rinse herself off. The bathtub is waiting for her next. The water is very pleasant, but she becomes concerned while soaking her body in it. What if she faints, she thinks to herself? The water is quite warm, the windows towards the private garden are fogged up because of the heat and the humidity. Nobody will even realize. She takes a breath and decides that this mindset must go and instead, something relaxing and joyful must replace it. Suddenly she has a smile on her face. She stretches herself out of the tub, in all her naked beauty, to reach for the window in front of her and wipe the misted glass clean. Once again, she allows herself to enjoy the beautiful, fashioned spa garden. Her entire mind and body relax. After they have taken their baths, they wait for dinner to be served in their personal guest room.

The floor is covered by a rectangular floor mat used in Japan called a Tatami. In the middle of their room is a low table, a closet to put the bedding into during the day, and a separate closet for clothing, luggage, and Yukata. That's it, nothing else. It is all about keeping the mind calm and uncluttered, allowing it to focus on the huge windows which expose the private garden with its plants, rocks, and lanterns. A maid serves them their dinner. They are unaccustomed to sitting on the floor to eat and as soon as the staff leaves the room, they enjoy straightening their legs under the table. They grin while looking at each other wearing the Yukata, thinking about being a newly married couple in a foreign country. After they finish dinner, an elderly woman enters the room, greeting them with some Japanese words while kneeling. She removes their plates and informs them, using gestures, that she will now prepare the futon that they will be sleeping on. She lays it directly on the tatami floor. As a young woman, she feels slightly embarrassed watching the elderly lady doing the task and not offering to help. From the perspective of the artisan, though, it's the work she is respected and paid for. She recognizes now that sometimes, not helping is a sign of admiration. A very strong storm breaks out during the night, and she finds the heavy raindrops falling on the roof to be extremely loud, bothersome, and scary. Like a child, she finds some fairytales entering her mind. Perhaps it's a Samurai maneuvering on the roof top? Okay, that's just the result of watching too many movies about Samurais and Ancient Japanese culture. She snuggles closer to her husband, feeling protected and comforted by his presence beside her, and drifts into a world of dreams and calm.

QUESTIONS

- How do you like to prepare and inform yourself before a trip?
- Do you love to go with the flow, or do you prefer to be in control?
- In which areas do you like to go with the flow and surrender the outcome?
- What is more helpful for you, having some intriguing information or some precautions?
- Do you find yourself taking over others' tasks because you feel guilty for some reason? Why do you feel this guilt?
- What movies of different cultures have influenced you in a positive way? Write them down on a list so you can watch them again.

Exploring different cultures gives you the opportunity to view religions other than your own. Being curious helps to broaden our worlds.

JAPAN HONEYMOON PART 3

She and her hubby want to visit the old parts of Japan as well. Kyoto is considered the cultural capital of Japan. There are numerous Buddhist temples, Shinto shrines, palaces, and gardens to see.

Shinto ("The way of the gods") is the indigenous faith of the Japanese people and is as old as Japan itself. Shinto and Buddhism are Japan's two major religions. Buddhist temples and Shinto shrines are different in their aesthetic and architectural appearances as well.

Shinto shrines usually have a large gate, a *torii*, at the entrance, often decorated in vermillion, guarded by statues in the form of foxes, dogs, or other animals. Temples tend to be a more reserved color on the outside, but the interior area dedicated to the Buddha is often filled with ornate gold statues and decorations. She and her hubby are very grateful to experience and observe how people practice their religions in such different ways. Their rituals invite us to receive. People typically pray silently at Buddhist temples, though occasionally, the more devout will chant mantras. It greatly impacts her life to see Japanese people of all ages so devout as they sit in front of a large incense burner and fan the smoke towards themselves for purification, while others take the blessing by walking quickly and reaching out their hand to caress the smoke in more of a drive-through fashion. The same occurs in the Shinto shrine; there are people who consciously visit the shrine while others love to just walk through and breathe in the scenery and nature. They want to be in the presence of something ancient and sacred. The visitors to the shrine wash their hands and mouths at a water basin before they enter. They must ring a bell and clap their hands to rouse the gods and pray. She witnesses a young couple receiving a blessing from the priest. It's a very special event, seeing another couple in the same phase of their lives as she and her hubby, recently choosing to go through life with their love companion. Zen is a branch of Japanese Buddhism. In Japan, the Zen temples have beautiful gardens, often with a pond or a lake, but also featuring the famous stone garden - often called a "Zen Garden" in the West. She is always fascinated by the pictures of those Zen gardens. For her they represent a place of calmness and peace. Of course, she has to visit one, having no doubt that this will be a sanctuary of tranquility. When she arrives, she sees the stone garden in front of her. With the assistance of a rake, the white gravel is neat and in order with a beautiful flow pattern. Suddenly, her meditative state is harshly interrupted. Out of the speakers next to her come loud announcements while pupils in their school uniforms arrive and flock the gardens. She doesn't expect such liveliness, especially not in this place. She realizes that the Japanese school system integrates objective lessons into their teachings; therefore, everywhere you go you will find students running around and chatting. Even though they are on their honeymoon and are not that eager on being confronted with a dark time in history, they decide to visit the Hiroshima Peace Memorial Museum. For them, visiting a foreign country includes gaining more perspective by broadening their views of the culture, its population, and its history. Even in the museum they are accompanied by a large group of pupils. It's not easy for her to grasp that the children don't require the support of a teacher while digesting the not only unpleasant, but scary exposition. For her it's important to see the world through a different lens, letting go of expectations, myths, and idealization, and instead confronting herself with what the truth is and giving herself the permission to feel and think whatever she is feeling and thinking in that very moment. There are moments of shade as well as moments of bright sunlight. Moments of sadness as well as moments of illumination.

QUESTIONS

- From whom do you like to get blessings?
- Are you giving yourself permission to bless yourself?
- How about your place of recovery - do you have one, or maybe more than one?
- What is so special about them, and in particular, meaningful to you?
- Do you love to create or visit places you can connect with? Do you have a variety of possibilities to choose from when needing to recharge yourself?
- What helps improve your mood and your confidence when life feels challenging?

There is still a sense of mysticism when someone introduces themselves as an artist. The world of an artist is associated with nearly everything and is often controversial, sometimes related to being unconventional, rebellious, independent, chaotic, rich, and full, wild, with no classification, with freedom, abundance and whatever else comes to your mind.

ART SCHOOL - CREATIVITY

She has had this dream of getting creative and attending a three-dimensional art class for some time. She and her hubby connected with their dreams, had a clear understanding of what they would like to experience in their lives, and decided to follow them, make them come alive.

Their goal was to live abroad, to live in Miami, to stay there for one year for further education and especially for her, to take the time to explore her additional skills outside that of being a therapist. She found a specific school, a private art school in Miami. The teacher there was a former art teacher at the University of Miami and is now the proud owner of his own art school. For her it's a great advantage that she gets credit for what she learned and even applied as a therapist at home before coming here. She used art and crafting as one of the tools to work with patients in the hospital and other facilities where she practiced therapy. It is very convenient that she doesn't have to start at the beginning again, and instead, is able to move on to the next level, by taking in his individual teaching.

The school is located on the second floor of a small industrial building. There is a ballet school on the same floor with all the young girls in their pink tutus either standing by the door or quickly running by to be on time for their lesson.

Expressions in different ways.

The door of the art school is open. She steps into the atelier for the first time. She finds herself in a creative surrounding where one huge room is divided into two departments, one for painting and one for sculpturing. The atmosphere is very indulging. On one side there are different kinds of stones, the metal tools and hammers, and on the other side, a pedestal with a naked model positioned for the students who have their canvases in front of them, ready to capture the lines and the shapes of the model with chalks or oil paint.

All the walls in this huge room are covered with paintings, sculptures and art pieces created by the art teacher. The shelves and special spots are filled with pieces of wood, metal, stones, vases, dried flowers, and other pieces discovered, one can imagine, while on travels through markets and old buildings in ancient parts of the world.

A room with mostly female artists from different countries and cultures. What a feast.

How is it possible to combine the different ways of expressing creativity in one room? Classical music is accompanying the painters while three-dimensional artists are working in stone and clay.

Here she is – a new fascinating world, a true treasure is opening up right in front of her eyes. It's such an unreal situation she has never considered she would ever be a part of.

The first thing she must do is train her eyes to be able to focus on "the points". The teacher returns regularly to monitor her and ensure she stays on track when he says, "Watch your points of reference!"

First, she creates a maquette out of clay so that she has a concrete reference for later, when she is upscaling into a bigger piece of art – a female torso.

It's tempting not to get distracted by the painters with their wonderful vivid oil colors against the monochrome colors of the stones.

She must learn to familiarize herself with the different characters of the compositions of the stone. How to include the veins of a stone and the unpredictable structure of a stone.

Her teacher shows her how she can approach the challenges with an unexpected solution: he shows her how to consciously chisel pieces away. She hears him say: *Yes, the stone – the art piece, could break into two pieces, therefore, be aware of the impact of each movement of the chisel and hammer; use the riffle and the files in an appropriate way.*

She loves the sensual touch of the different tools which are used in sculpturing.

The different kinds and sizes of the chisels, the riffles, and files.

For her it's so fascinating to explore the right balance between the proportion of the tools, the weight, and the grip of holding them.

Finding the right balance between the impact, the intention, the focus, the power and the softness.

It's so revitalizing for her to learn new skills, skills which are needed to hear the chisel connecting with the hammer and the art piece. It's like witnessing a conversation between them.

Yes, she loves to connect with all her senses. To touch a stone can be such a sensual experience – she loves it. To use the tips of her fingers to explore the surface is as important as using her eyes.

It's not about either/or, it's the combination of the two which creates the best result.

Sometimes, even her sense of smell is activated, especially if the stone includes sulfur.

The most challenging part for her is to choose to either leave it raw, create a silky finish, or even polishing it to have a shiny effect at the end.

It's a step-by-step process and it takes time. Everlasting endurance is asked of her. Connecting with the stone helps her to not give up.

Her clothes are full of stone dust, her hair has some strands of stone powder on it, and her face has some traces of stone- the make-up of a sculptor. She feels like an artist... Yes, she is an artist. She gets reminded by her teacher, who has a kind but demanding way of teaching, to take a step back to observe the piece overall, not focusing only on detail but also on the bigger picture.

Every small change in the silhouette is influencing the surface, and vice versa.

She reflects: to be the creator of a piece of art is like being pregnant. Feeling the doubts, the uncertainty of what's coming, unsure of yourself and your new creation, and then the excitement when it's born, to then letting go, knowing inside that you have to release your creation so it can become whatever it is meant to be. What satisfaction.

QUESTIONS

- Independence, where would you like to experience this?
- What is an almost unreal, barely reachable dream or goal you never gave yourself the space to try or even had the guts to think about, but would love to have in your life and be a part of? Write it down, use images and words for it.
- Where would you like to live one day, even if it's just for one month, perhaps a year or even several years?
- How would you like to live there? Visualize it with all your senses.
- What would you like to experience in this lifetime?
- What do you like to create with your own hands?
- What excites you and makes your heart sing?
- Now it's the time to make your "dream list" – your "heart list". Get creative.

There are times when an artist likes to be alone, to work like a hermit, to be surrounded only by their materials and tools, and the stillness. Sometimes music is welcomed too. Just to be alone with the creations they bring forth from their inner worlds, their emotions. As in any other field of life, there are sequences in which it makes sense to sit back, be quieter and more introverted. The opposite is true as well. You need to be extroverted when life demands that you step out and show up. That's balance.

ART EXHIBITION

She, as an artist, is fully into creation, whether she is creating an art piece for a friend, a special order from a client or building a concept for an exhibition. Sometimes it's an event on her own or with others. She likes to campaign together with other painters. It can be good synergy to have paintings together with sculptures in the same room.

The paintings are often displayed on walls and the sculptures in open spaces, on the floor or a pedestal, or hanging from the ceiling.

Another wonderful experience is gathering with other sculptors. They all follow the same theme, but everyone expresses themselves in a unique way, choosing different stones, using materials that are suitable for creating sculptures and three-dimensional artwork.

The challenge of a group exhibition is that every artist has their own personality and preference on how and where their art piece must be presented.

Whether it's a very private exhibition or larger ones in and outdoors, with a performance artist included. She loves it all.

She challenges herself by taking up space for herself and her art pieces. To step up and out is an act of defiance. She is neither offended by critique nor does she rely on compliments from visitors, guests, or the other artists. It is a claim to becoming comfortable with her own truth.

She is always excited and a bit nervous when she shows her creations to the public for the first time.

Another challenge with attending exhibitions is the pricing of the art pieces. She needs to be comfortable with the prices she is asking for. Getting the pricing right can be emotional, which is quite upsetting to her. There are many things she must consider outside of the actual hours it took to create those sculptures using chisels, hammers, riffles and files. She must include the time and process of finding the idea, shopping for the stone and the rent of the atelier. Another thing not to be forgotten is the bases which are made from metal or wood. These must be specifically produced for each piece, even including a cost to hire someone to install the heavier sculptures in a secure way at times. There are so many steps included in this process.

Creativity will always include some levels of entitlement, which is not always clearly understood or acknowledged.

It is the same as finding one's own unique manifestation of living the life one wants to live.

To get creative is often the process of having a calling, a vision. While she walks through the hall where all the different kind of stones lie, waiting to be chosen, it often feels like a stone speaks to her and whispers, *Just take me*. She adores this connection. Some have this connection with an animal, with flowers, with colors, with different canvases, with fabrics, or with fruits and vegetables.

Life becomes all-embracing the moment someone is open enough to receive. For her it is like a certain energy which she can sense.

The conversation she has with the stones are often quite special: *Please appreciate my appearance, don't try to fix me, find peace with my irregularity.* The interaction goes on: *Help, I am nature, one-hundred-percent natural; I am not created in a test tube, I have my own personality, my own spirit. If you are open, I will guide you, I will tell you where to chip away, I will reveal where you must alter the line to have a flow which perfectly matches the entire sculpture.* She is captivated by the conversation with the stone. She is the co-creator with the stone and its energy. To be able to use all of her senses is blissful and precious to her. When the day comes to let go of one of her pieces, she is happy knowing that the new owner, through this creation of art, will receive great positive energy in their home. To share happiness is so fulfilling.

QUESTIONS

- What is art to you?
- What kind of art do you love and appreciate?
- How important is it to you to express yourself or to dive into someone else's way of creativity?
- Are you able to appreciate what you create?
- How about your inner critic? How do you quiet that voice?
- What are some situations in your daily life where you find yourself being more introverted, and where do you find yourself being more extroverted?
- In what area of your life would you love to give your inner artist permission to fully step up and be unstoppable? What would this look like?

A lot of people feel a force of attraction towards dolphins. Perhaps this is because they have seen them on television, heard about their soft nature, how they care for their young, and how sociable they are in the way they connect with each other. Is this social interaction what most of us as humans are longing for as well? The feelings one experiences when you are that close to these beautiful, graceful animals is nearly too phenomenal to put into words. She is overcome with emotion and gratitude.

CONNECTIONS WITH DOLPHINS

Living in Miami, she considers visiting a dolphin research center. For her it's important that it is not only an attraction for guests and tourists, but also, more preferably, focuses on the wellbeing of the dolphins too. In the morning it's only open for clients with autism and other therapeutic needs. The therapy provides an unforgettable sensory experience, and they go there to have uninterrupted time with the dolphins and to work with the specialist therapists. The earnings and donations from the guests, who visit in the afternoon, keep the dolphin center going. This ensures that people with disabilities get the best possible treatment and that those fascinating creatures live in a safe environment and receive the best available care.

When she and her hubby step into the center, she notices several tanks and pools which all lead to a channel, and from there, lead out into the open sea. Every tank has a bottlenose dolphin calmly swimming around in it. She is amazed by how large they are. The water isn't that clear because it's the water from the sea, but still, she can see them from the deck. It's a controversial inner conflict for her because on the one hand there is the depravity of liberty, but on the other hand, other assistance animals such as epilepsy dogs come to her mind. They are in service for humans, too.

First, they get an educational briefing about these interesting and intelligent mammals. One of the standards of the center is that no matter whether the dolphins play with the guests or not, or if they are not in the mood for entertaining, they still get the same treatment and portions of food. There are some toys in the water and if they want to play, great, and if not, that's also fine. This respect towards the animals gives her such a good feeling about going into the water to join them. The center also provides a channel for the dolphins to go out into the sea and return whenever they would like to. They explain that every dolphin has its own character. The males like to stay out at sea for quite some time while the females, who are a little more shy, swim out more briefly. There's a wonderful energy of trust from being treated well. She marvels at the wonderful connection between the staff and the dolphins. The staff explain that the animals can detect and will swim directly towards a person who has a medical issue, and even point at it with their nose. They are told that they should never approach the dolphin from the front and to the head. Dolphins do not like to be touched on the head and on their blowholes. To do so would evoke the powerful flukes of the dolphin.

She and her hubby are invited to go into a cage together with their fins, masks and snorkels on. They swim as they are told, with their arms close to the sides of their bodies, remaining close to the cage until they become accustomed to the murky water created by the algae. They make some adjustments to their equipment. Suddenly she hears a click sound, and *voilà*! Here she is, a beautiful female dolphin coming from the bottom of the natural pool towards them. She forgets to breathe. What a phenomenal experience. To echolocate objects nearby, dolphins produce high-frequency clicks. These clicks create sound waves that travel quickly through the water around them.

The dolphin swims side by side her and her hubby, watching to see what they are up to. They get some instructions from the staff to entertain the animal. They say it sometimes works to make a human wheelbarrow, to get the dolphins attention. One must be in front of the other, holding on to the legs of the partner in front and pushing them forward by using the fins. Yes, it works. The dolphin enjoys it. She and her hubby are now in a circus, or dolphinarium. Only the other way around; they are now there to entertain the animal. A marvel.

She has a different experience with dolphins at another time in her life, this time in another part of Florida. It's on an island that has very rich vegetation, avenues of palm trees as far as the eye can see, and a large variety of flowers and plants. The beach is remarkable. The sandy beach has shells in all different colors and sizes spread all over the tropical nirvana. It must be the capital of the shell empire.

Their vacation continues in this wonderful paradise. The clear and intense blue water of the sea is so inviting. She loves to take walks along the beach, feeling the sand between her toes. She hears someone calling, "Watch the dolphins swimming by!" She instantly gazes at them and begins to run along the beach while calling out towards them in the hope that they come back to her. Without thinking, she gets into the water all the way up to her hips. She cannot believe her eyes when they turn around and head back towards her, talking to her without words, saying, *If you want to connect with us, here we are.* Her heart is racing with so much gratitude, having those pods of wild dolphins so near to her. No guides, no motorboats to play with, no food, nothing. It's only her and this unconditional love and interest for each other. What an unforgettable moment. Total bliss.

QUESTIONS

- What is your approach towards animals?
- Do they get your love without fulfilling your expectations?
- Whom should be a delight for whom, animals for humans, or vice versa?
- Does it satisfy you to look after and care for animals on a regular daily basis, or perhaps only occasionally, like dog-sitting or cat care?
- If you were an animal, what kind of animal would you like to be?
- What fascinates you about this animal? What qualities do you see in it, and which of those do you recognize in yourself?
- Perhaps you should get a photo of this animal for the background on one of your devices, to remind you of these qualities?

How important are animals in your life? Do you have a connection to or even a special attraction towards a specific species? I love to talk to animals. This might seem strange to you, but for me it's such a fun and mystical way of connecting with other beings. Some people sing to their cows to have them draw closer to them. Do you believe that all creatures of nature have feelings, and yearn for appreciation in one way or the another?

CONNECTIONS WITH WILD ANIMALS

She isn't sure where this gift for connecting with animals came from. She is not some sort of professional animal whisperer. Still, there is something special that happens when she is out in nature. When she walks or hikes somewhere, her eyes will magically move in a certain direction. When she's not even trying to see an animal, she will often spot a majestic eagle circling high up in the air, or a vulture spreading its wings, a squirrel jumping playfully from one tree to another, or a woodpecker with his red feathers, a deer with beautiful big eyes. She has, of course, with her hubby, been to a national park without spotting an animal, maybe one or two butterflies were floating around, but that was it. It's very interesting to notice that if she isn't eagerly trying to catch sight of something, that often the wonders appear. It's as if she gives the animals the freedom to show up should they wish to. She reflects on this. It's similar to her daily life. Whenever she is relaxed and going with the flow, positive things and surprises show up. To have such an easy-going connection to wild animals is wonderfully refreshing and moving for her. Her senses are very distinct. Whether it's a small movement in the corner of her eye, or a swish somewhere close to her, she will turn in the direction she senses it. It's like the energy changes. When she makes contact, she attempts to connect. From a flock of chamois running up a hill, a capricorn with impressive horns, or a proud stag with large antlers, she, with a softened but natural tone, will talk to them. She tells the animal how beautiful it is, and what she sees in the animal. It is also important to her to introduce her hubby by name, if he is with her. Yes, perhaps this seems bizarre or odd, but it sparks real joy, to have conversations like this with animals. She does not worry about what others may think. Is it not better to share the respect and love we have for humans with animals? They, too, deserve this. She is attuned to the gifts life brings her. She turns up the volume of being able to receive the magnificent gifts and allows herself to experience different ways of communicating, verbally and energetically, with both humans and animals.

Instead of conforming to the norm, she chooses to experience life to the fullest, on nature's terms.

QUESTIONS

- Is there or has there been a wild animal with whom you have had a special connection?
- What kind of animal was it? Perhaps it wasn't an animal. Was there something else in nature you felt a similar connection to?
- Why do or did you feel so attracted to it?
- What was so precious about it?
- What kind of animal would you still like to connect with?
- How do you communicate with animals? In a verbal or non-verbal way?
- Would you like to explore improving non-verbal communication with them?
- Are you ready to become more receptive to nature, by choosing to open your eyes and ears to the unexpected?

Curiosity and interest can take us a long and exciting way. Perhaps you remember a situation in your life when you told yourself never ever, but still felt drawn towards it? This often happens to her. It starts before it even begins. She is preparing for a challenge in India. Starting at an adventure shop, she gets everything she requires for this project. Why don't you join her?

INDIA PART 1 - PREPARATION FOR THE VISION QUEST

It is only after the long flight that she will get to meet the other seekers. Most of them are coming in from England to Mumbai in India. The group, named The Seekers of the Vision Quest, will be together for two weeks.

She got to know the guide who will be leading the tour about three months ago. He was a yoga and mantra teacher from England, giving a workshop at the retreat center in Mallorca. She attended a therapeutic education seminar, and he was there to teach yoga and mantra chanting. Outwardly curious, she was invited to a session in his group. She was inquisitive, which he liked a lot. As if receiving a wild card, he offered her the opportunity to join him and some of his students for a vision quest to India. He enjoyed her questions so much that he didn't care that she did not have any of the prerequisites, such as experience with yoga. She wasn't even able to sit on the floor for long periods of time. The teacher was open to having her hubby join her on the trip. He said it's always a positive contribution to the experience if the spouse of a participant takes part, as it will create alignment between the two of them.

She was confused, overwhelmed and didn't know what to think about this offer from a stranger. Deciding whether they should go to India and travel with him and his students to certain areas, in an unfamiliar country, or whether they should stay at home, choosing the comfort of certainty, was a real challenge for the couple. She had never considered visiting India before. Her concerns were always that it would be too loud, too crowded, too filthy, too extreme, too chaotic, too many beggars, along with the discomfort of how overwhelming the poverty would be. But having the opportunity to travel accompanied by a spiritual guide who lives in India most of the year was too good to miss.

Taking the opportunity to explore new territory together was comforting. At least they would have each other for support. It's such a relief to have this kind of mindset: If anything goes wrong, there is always a solution, they can just catch a plane home.

A few weeks before the event, she receives the packing list.

She would love to take a lot of things with her, just in case, but not this time. She can't because they will have to carry their luggage around. For practical reasons, the guide recommends a backpack. Next stop is a visit to the outdoor equipment store. The personal quest has begun. While a store clerk shows them a variety of backpacks, she can't help noticing the mosquito nets. She must decide between the triangular or the rectangular one. She loves the rectangular net because it has more space above and its shaped like a box. The added space will give her the feeling of being able to breathe, compared to the triangular one, which narrows at the top. She knows that she must take care of her needs and is aware that this will alleviate her fear, anxiety and claustrophobia.

The packing list also shows the amount of clothes they will need for the whole quest. Because they will be in Ashrams most of the time, white clothes are recommended. She never wears white; she feels as though she looks so unhealthy in it. White clothes are not easy to find in wintertime in Europe, and they are not easy to wash, but they are more comfortable in the warm climate. The clothes must also be loose enough so that she and her hubby are able to sit down on the floor.

The list goes on: a light sleeping bag, a spoon and knife, a water bottle, enough toilet paper, soap, candles and even a torch (for when the electricity goes off), underwear, and a shawl to cover up. She takes some lice-repellant powder to spread on the mattresses. Her saying: Rather be safe than sorry.

She can sense that this trip is going to be more challenging than most. Especially since she prefers nice hotels or guesthouses on her vacations. There won't be any luxury on this trip. Only the basics, such as a bed, a shower, and a toilet, perhaps a chair and a table too. Vision quests are different for everyone.

Thinking about being at Mumbai's airport, waiting to spot her and her hubby's luggage, brings a smile to her face. She is still at home, but her imagination is already there. Spotting the two backpacks on the conveyor belt will be easy because they are in huge plastic bags to make sure that the handles don't get caught up in the roll band of the luggage. She has marked them with pink dots like a Dalmatian dog. She occasionally loves to be a little crazy and creative.

They plan to put the pink-dotted plastic bags underneath the mattresses so they can connect the beds together, to close the gap and ensure that no bugs get too cozy with them. Her spouse knows her well, but still, he gets nervous when she is in a "no matter what" state. In this state, there are no fear or worries in her universe, only ease and freedom. He loves her vitality, the way she expresses herself. Everything is intense in her universe: the sunshine and the ease, the thoughtfulness and the doubts. Her mission is to live a life of multiplicity rather than mediocrity.

QUESTIONS

- Are you curious about life? Rate your curiosity from 1 to 10. 1 being not a lot to 10 being extremely.
- Would you like to expand your curiosity and inquisitiveness?
- Are you clear about your needs? What must you have in order to support yourself and minimize your fear, anxiety or claustrophobia?
- What is your attitude towards difficult and challenging situations?
- Do you have a optimistic approach such as a slogan like, *Every problem has a solution*?
- What is your own personal mantra you use to encourage yourself?
- When going through life, are you very cautious or more impulsive?
- Do you ever find yourself in a "no matter what: state?
- When and where would you like to use "no matter what" more often?
- Can you remember when last you were in the "no matter what" state?

Lifehack: Instead of mediocrity, give yourself permission to live your life in multiplicity, abundance, and diversity. You are worthy of it!

India is calling. It's very helpful to be accompanied by a group and a guide who are familiar with the culture, the habits, and the spiritual approach of the quest. Do you choose to slip into your white clothes to walk a spiritual path, even if it's only for a short amount of time? Yes. Sandals are practical, too.

INDIA PART 2 - STARTING THE VISION QUEST

Arriving at Mumbai after a long flight and spotting their backpacks in their pink-dotted plastic bags is such a relief. With the backpack on her back, she looks for a toilet to change out of her civilian clothes into her white vision-quest clothes. What a pleasant surprise when they discover there are European toilets too – some familiarity to start with. It's easy to identify the other participants because they are all dressed in white and most of them have a fair skin tone, like her. The teacher, a spiritual master and mantra yogi, arrives dressed in orange, and looks vastly similar to – with long white hair pulled into a bun and a pointed white beard – the wise Dumbledore from Harry Potter.

A short welcome to everyone and off they go. A bus is already waiting for them just outside the airport. Noise, dust, and a wave of hot air comes towards her. They get into the car. The journey to their inner soul has started, and they don't know what to expect.

The horn of the bus is used so often that she wonders if driving in this traffic is safe at all. Different countries have different rules and habits. After a while, she understands that using the horn while driving in India is so necessary.

They arrive at their first Ashram, just outside the pulsing city, close to the sea. Exotic flowers and birds combine with the smells of different spices.

The teacher gives her and her hubby one of the biggest rooms, because they are a couple. They even have their own bathroom and two normal beds. Nothing fancy, but still much more luxurious compared to the other students, who have beds made from cement, a thin mattress, and showers and bathrooms that they must share.

She is very grateful for this consideration from the teacher. She knows there are a lot of challenges awaiting her. All the other participants have either been to India before or have attended several yoga and mantra retreats. For her and her hubby, everything is new, which is very clear from the moment they eat their first meal. Sitting down on the ground, no one really talks while they eat, and afterwards, they all go to an area where everyone cleans and washes their dishes with a piece of soap made from cow dung. It's a disinfectant, they say.

In the meditation room there are carpets on the floor and some pictures of the gurus of the Ashram on the walls. The smell of the incense pervades the entire room. The atmosphere of inner peace and the energy of the sounds of the mantra takes over in a pleasant way.

To prevent her feet and legs from cramping while sitting on the floor, she makes use of a lot of cushions. It is more comfortable and helps her to sit upright.

The teacher has injured his shoulder, but some of the participants who are also yoga teachers lead the way.

She learns the difference between singing and chanting, how to chant the diverse mantras, their meaning, and how to integrate them into daily life to access their mental and physical power. Not every mantra is used for the same purpose.

She loves to chant. It helps her to connect with her inner world, her soul, and brings peace to her mind. In addition, she feels it improves her awareness and concentration.

The main goal of this quest is to discover the transformational tools for

self-understanding, spiritual insights, and practical methods for uplifting one's quality of life.

After spending a few days in the same place to acclimate, it's now time to explore another spiritual locale and Ashram. This one is more of a guesthouse, and it is close to the holy mountain called Arunachala. It's located in an area where there are a lot of fields and nothing around them but open space. Again, they are given very nice accommodation, a bedroom, and a separate bathroom. The roof is made out of straw and the walls of clay. They must share the room with a small bat. Luckily a mosquito net is already installed above the bed. She realizes that if she has to get up during the night to go to the toilet she will be exposed to the bat. She asks herself: Is this my own fear or one I have been taught? Often the fear of something isn't even hers. She took it in from somewhere, but up until now, as if it were her own truth, she has restricted herself because of someone else's beliefs. That is such a realization for her. To always question the fear. She knows she must be open minded but not naïve, not taking everything in as "the" truth, not even from her teacher.

Other important parts of the quest besides the chanting are the teachings of the Nadis, the Chakras, and the different breathing techniques.

She really struggles, especially when she must hold her breath for a long time. She is reminded of the times she had allergic reactions, suffocation seizures, and had to be rushed to the emergency room.

She gives herself allowances to do the breathing exercises for as long as she feels comfortable with.

Being in an environment like this, a small Ashram with small spaces, is distressing to her. Sitting together after the teaching, having a chat, and watching how the family cooks the vegetarian food for the whole group is relaxing. Doing the laundry in the colorful plastic bins, hanging the clean, white clothes outside between the huts to dry, is a nice activity to give her mind some rest.

Every day they go to the Sri Ramana Ashram, where there are peacocks and monkeys walking around. All their shoes are taken off before the entrance and put into their bag to make sure they still have them after their visit. Because their guide is a spiritual teacher and a famous mantra guru, she and the whole group get the exclusive opportunity to chant in the main meditation hall. The floor is made from white marble and sitting on it is very cooling. It's such a gift to cool down and be afforded such a rare opportunity to chant in this sacred place. She is humbled to have this privilege. There are no thoughts, no time, only being in the present and being part of this energy, which is in her and around her. Such bliss.

Wherever she looks around she sees herself in contrast. Whether it's during the short ride on the tuk-tuk into the nearby city to visit the huge Ashram, the meditation hall or visiting the market. She finds a way to become comfortable with being confronted with beggars everywhere she goes. She gives money if she feels she wants to, otherwise she gives them heartfelt greetings, and sometimes even ignores them if needed. It's not an easy task finding the balance between being kind to others and being kind to herself as well.

QUESTIONS

- What helps you to connect easily with your inner self, your soul, and brings peace to your mind?
- Do you include breathing exercises, mantra chanting, or just singing in your daily routines?
- Do you have a spiritual teacher or a mentor for your own personal growth?
- Where do you make adaptions even to an expert's suggestion, because you trust your gut and you know that whatever it is, it is right for you and is your truth?
- In which areas of your life do you still restrict yourself because of the opinion of someone else?
- Are you aware of where in your life you have bought into someone else's story and opinion?
- How kind are you to yourself?

A Power Hack: Just be in the question, and ask yourself: Is this my truth?

It is often helpful to write down or talk about exploring and experiencing new things. To have someone listen to our thoughts and emotions can be very insightful and relieving. Being on the train through India could be just a ride on a train but it could also be a train ride that brings you closer to you. If you allow it to, your awareness and self-actualization can be unlocked through these experiences.

INDIA PART 3 - EXPLORATION

On the way to the train station, they make a stop to get their survival pack. Recommended by their guide, this pack includes water, bananas, nuts, and other snacks. It's all safe, convenient to carry, ready to eat, and filling.

Whenever they walk by or drive by a stand selling coconuts, they stop to hydrate themselves. It's fascinating to watch how the vendor opens the

green coconuts, which have a softer outer husk and inner shell compared to the harder brown ones. He pops off the top of the coconut with a knife, cuts into and around the area that was covered with the petal and serves it with a drinking straw. She loves this refreshing coconut water. It's quite confusing to see how everyone just throws the empty coconuts on the floor because she is so used to waste separation at home.

Several hours of traveling by train await her. The whole group gathers with their luggage and must wait because the train is delayed. Some sit on the floor but she prefers to sit on her backpack. She worries about how she will handle the lack of air-conditioning with the amount of people on the train and the heat. Well, hopefully there will be some fans.

Like the saying goes, You haven't been to India until you've taken a ride on an Indian train. She knows that in most parts of the world, people are used to this sort of travel, or worse. Her life has been one of privilege. Her guide has organized tickets for the "sleeper class" with simple beds. They are wooden benches with a padded surface, six on one side of the aisle and two on the other. During the day, the middle beds are folded down flat against the compartment walls to allow passengers to sit on the lower beds. There's no privacy in the sleeper class but that's not a problem because they travel during the daytime. It's an opportunity for her, her hubby, and the whole group to interact with the locals from all walks of life. The windows of the train are opened fully to circulate the air, and this allows her to glimpse out into the incredible natural Indian beauty, lush greenery, and rural villages. She is so proud that she is able to surrender to the situation right now.

After the train trip, they must hop on a bus which will take them to another Ashram. This one is located close to the mountains.

This time her hubby must be a craftsman. Their room has no wardrobe or nails put into the walls for their mosquito net. He must find a way to drill four nails into the cement wall. This is a challenge. With patience and endurance, the mission is successfully executed. What a victory! He is her hero. They feel like a powerful couple because they support and motivate each other. This understanding is such a contribution to their quest.

They have daily teachings. For her it's challenging to see how her teacher compares himself with others, not even trying to hold back with his opinion and judgement about the broken Indian system and their lack of spiritual knowledge. She finds his arrogance unbearable. She even has thoughts about leaving, already knowing where the nearest airport is to get a flight back home. How can she feel comfortable when she is being triggered by him and his statements? She has an upcoming phone call with a friend of hers back home. Her friend will be more objective because she isn't as involved as her and her hubby right now. She finds comfort in knowing she can share and express her feelings and perplexity and know that her friend will hold the space for her. What a great friendship. To have people who she can go to, and vice versa, is an important quality in her life. She feels more relaxed after the call. Sometimes a chat with another woman is helpful. But it is very liberating to know she has the support from her hubby too. She can let go of whatever isn't hers to carry. Return to sender! The same holds true for meditation. She is with a teacher who can meditate for several hours, but kindness, open-mindedness, and foresight aren't noticeable in his character. Is there only one truth?

She remembers a joke: Two people get together; one says to the other: "Oh, I desperately have to tell you about how I lost my ego!" This brings a smile to her face. All this about the ego, and then to have to try to lose it, no matter what? Everyone has an ego. She is so tired of hearing people tell her how much more advanced they are than she is. She prefers to just acknowledge that she has one, and it's sometimes more potent and other times less present. She would rather uphold her self-love and radical self-acceptance than stress out or be that tightly wound up by trying to lose it. Everything is a process.

QUESTIONS

- Do you see you and your partner or spouse as a powerful couple?
- Where and when the most?
- Do you love to support and motivate people around you? Does this energize you too?
- How about asking for support for yourself?
- In which areas are you already open to being vulnerable and asking for help and advice?
- Where do you enjoy exploring opportunities to receive additional support?
- Are you at peace, even though you know that you still have a long way to go?
- What qualities do you possess that you are proud of?

What a wonderful gift it is for us humans to be able to move in water, where the body becomes weightless and it's effortless to change positions. The water even entices adults to be playful again, to splash, feel free to swim around, dive under or turn on their back and just use their hands to stabilize their floating bodies. Swimming can be so energizing, refreshing, and rejuvenating. Why don't you swim and perhaps sing along?

TO SWIM

She loves swimming and she does it in her own unique way; perhaps like a duck would describe it best, but who's checking. It's a normal breaststroke with her head above the water. She often gets some neck and lower back pain if she swims in this position too long. Looking around fascinates her. While swimming in the lake, she enjoys watching the ducks with their cute flappers passing by, or Eurasian coots, who can dive down to six meters deep and return to the surface in a completely different, unexpected place. She watches the boats pass by the nature around her, looking at the beautiful blue sky and the formation of the clouds, all the while being able to socialize, have a chat with her hubby or a friend, while moving and being refreshed in the water. When she swims out into the sea, she likes to look at the horizon and the waves that come towards her. On her way back to shore she observes the beach, its colorful beach huts, and the people who walk by or the salespeople who sell ice cream, clothes, or other goods. To be in water recharges her and helps her to connect to her inner child and opens her up to a playful and carefree world. In water she feels whole.

A friend of hers gives her the name of a good swimming instructor to improve her breaststroke and crawl technique. She and her swimming trainer get along very well. The trainer is a former professional gymnast but is qualified to give swimming lessons in every discipline. She loves to teach children and adults alike to enjoy swimming and gain more confidence and ease with it. This is more about adapting the right body posture, competent arm and leg movements and breathing methods, as well as to swim long distances without any neck or back pain. By nature, she is more a speedboat than a float, and her instructor must slow her down because she hyperventilates and gets worn out too fast. To find the balance between action and stillness is the right approach for improved performance. When she swims in the lake on her own, she uses a red buoy like the one from the movie Baywatch. Only this time she isn't wearing the sexy red swimsuit. It's a black tankini, to better ensure that everything stays in place.

She is certain she will use those two techniques, and if needed, when accompanied by someone to have a conversation, laughter or even a jubilant cheer with, she can rely on the duck dance. To swim and change between the different swimming styles gives her freedom and joy. Developing new skills is like adding more colors to her paint palette called life. It's her freedom to choose, whatever and whenever she wants to.

QUESTIONS

- Do you love water? Do you like to swim and play around in water?
- What natural element are you most attracted to?
- What makes you feel connected to this element?
- What is a metaphor for it?
- Do you use sport to get in touch with this element?
- What kind of sport or activity is it?
- Is it to boost your energy level, increase muscle mass and flexibility, or is it more recreational?
- What new skills do you like to learn, by either watching on YouTube or in nature, or exploring by doing?
- How do you find the balance between action, stillness, and rest?

Does this situation sound familiar to you: When getting prepared for a certain adventure or a daily event, something suddenly unexpectedly alters your focus. How do you react? Do you consider looking at it or do you vehemently push it away? Do you ever ask yourself: What will this create for me right now, or one or three years from now, if…? Will it bring more into my life? Why don't you put on your swim cap and come with me! It doesn't matter if it's a fancy one or a plainly colored one, it's about being ready for the experience.

TO SWIM: SURPRISE

This morning while she stands in front of the swimming pool, wearing a swimsuit and her pink swimming cap, mentally and physically preparing herself for another swimming lesson, her teacher introduces her to a friend of hers who lost her adult son. On the recommendation of her instructor, they start having a conversation. The scenery is quite awkward.

Here she stands with her cellulite and curvy curves besides the swimming pool and in front of this mother who is in mourning. Suddenly it's not about the daily body shaming anymore, it's about real life. This mom heard that she is a sculptor and a therapist. What a great combination for her situation and for her deepest wish to have the right person create a sculpture for her son for the graveyard. It will be a family gravestone. Yes, she is an artist, but she has never done work like this before. Two of her friends come to mind. She could ask them if they would like to create such an art piece. Stop! Her inner procrastinating mind chatter stops. She hears herself asking herself: *Why don't you take this great opportunity and this possibility to do something complex and creative? Instead, you've already thought of someone else who is more experienced with this kind of work and could do it, perhaps better?* Where does this low self-esteem come from? Why isn't she confident enough to take the gift the universe is offering to her? She realizes that she and no one else is meant to do it; the connection with the grieving mother is already there, and her new potential client is more than convinced that she will be the one to help her through the grieving process and to help her express her love for her son in an art piece. Yes, sometimes it's not how someone is dressed up or how they present themselves, like her with her swimming cap, but instead what energy, what heart quality, and presence comes from the person.

It's such a great experience to go with the mom and her other son through the entire process of creation. Several steps are required. First, getting into all the emotions, gathering their thoughts and ideas, then creating a model and sketches followed by the actual creation of the piece out of plaster, which will later be cast into bronze. After the art piece is poured into bronze, together with the casters, she creates the desired "Patina", the shades of colors of the bronze, using a blowtorch which helps to heat up the bronze and enhance the chemical reactions. The chemicals may be sprayed or brushed onto the hot metal surface. Magic happens right before her eyes, and the right color composition is created.

The art piece: Two vast hands made out of bronze, positioned on a stable base made out of stone, softly connected to each other. What a gift to be chosen as a supportive part of something so deeply emotional, being invited into the world of another family, experiencing their trust and the belief that she has the skills to transmit their feelings into a visible expression. Pure connection from her heart to theirs, and the other way around.

QUESTIONS

- What kind of grief have you experienced in your life?
- What was important for you in those times of mourning?
- What helped you in those situations?
- What advice would you give to your younger self on how to cope with sorrow, emotional pain, and sadness?
- Can you express your feelings and emotions?
- Are you in allowance with all your emotions?
- Are you capable of and ready to let go of the past and the heaviness it sometimes brings?
- Would you also like to express yourself in a creative way?
- What kind of expression would be a great fit for you?

Are you tempted to listen to others and their opinions, or their worries, before you brave an adventure? Or do you stay strong and confident and listen to your intuition? To look at the sky and become centered, without any thoughts or worries: every human being longs for moments like this, to not be stuck in the past or in the future, all the while missing the spark of the present. Let's be a bird who explores the wind and the free fall.

SKYDIVING

She heard from a good friend of hers how fascinating skydiving is. She has never considered jumping out of an airplane or helicopter, but before she knows it, she finds herself organizing this adventure for her and her hubby. Is it about taking a risk? She will soon find out.

Is there a special occasion she has dreamed of which is becoming a reality? Their tenth wedding anniversary was that dream.

While driving to the location where the challenge would take place, not really knowing what to expect, an air of nervousness fills the car. They arrive and park on the landing spot; it's a huge green field. Parking and stepping out of the car into the fresh air of the mountains combined with the awareness of the upcoming experience is liberating for them. They receive their safety briefing and their yellow filthy-reared oversized jumpsuits. She realizes the filth on the rear end is from landing and sliding along the grass landing spot.

There's still time to cancel the whole thing.

People have told her it's too dangerous, but she has always been of the belief that if it's time for her to leave the planet, it's time.

A thought pops into her head while she, her hubby, and the two instructors are heading in a small bus to the base of the helicopters. She hopes that none of the instructors have gone through a break-up recently and is planning to end their lives today.

Her heart rate goes up when she spots the engines of the birds of the air lying in wait, ready to fly. A rescue helicopter is there too, and interesting thoughts arise. One last visit to the bathroom.

She is excited, but her hubby is even more excited. Electricity is flowing everywhere.

She puts on her goggles and safety-wear and is connected to the instructor. They take their places on a bench-like back seat. Because it's a tandem flight, her instructor sits with his legs wide apart and she between him. Contrary to what you might think, there is no sexual energy in this kind of situation. It's all professional and there is no time for such thoughts or feelings. While it is very close, she knows that her and her hubby have trust and neither worry about being in such proximity to a stranger in this situation. Her instructor double checks that her goggles and safety harness are perfectly connected to him and his gear. This closeness would be really awkward in daily life, but not in these special circumstances. She takes a deep breath in. The engine starts up, the noise is tremendous, the vibration and power of this air-bird's moving rotors is so overwhelming. Even though she can see fear in his eyes, looking into her hubby's eyes gives her the comfort she needs. They have already decided that it is okay should either one of them choose not to jump, even if the helicopter is already in the air. What freedom. With this kind of acceptance, a lot more is possible. The door besides her hubby is opened, the fresh air from 4000m altitudes circulates through the entire aircraft. Her nerves are shot. It's so loud she can hardly hear anything. Her husband and his instructor slide towards the edge of the seat. In a second, her hubby is out of sight.

In one moment he was there and in another he was gone, taken by the wind.

Now it's her turn, the same procedure. She slides to the edge of the seat, her head tucked into the instructor's neck, jump and roll. Trying to take a deep breath is challenging. The pressure of the air on her skin makes it impossible to scream.

Freefall for 30 seconds.

Time stands still while in the freefall. No time, no thoughts, no worries – nothing. Only space, freedom and bliss. Only seconds, but it feels like infinity. The parachute is pulled and with drastic intensity, the freefall is interrupted. It feels as though someone is pulling her up towards heaven. What a feeling. She can now scream, and if her instructor was in front of her, he would be deaf. Instead, he is happy that his guest is experiencing so much joy. She can't stop laughing.

To see everything from this perspective fascinates her. The mission is not yet complete. With some spirals, her guide speeds up to catch her hubby so that they are on the same level and can see each and give some declaration of love to one another. What a moment, filled with so much gratitude. The landing is quite easy. She is in a sitting position, legs straight out in front, while the instructor behind her is kneeling and both are sliding softly over the grass until they come to a halt. She gets disconnected from the safety harness and the instructor. She only wants to see her hubby, but she lies in the grass and feels the earth beneath her. To put this kind of trust in others and herself has been enlightening. What a gift to be in this kind of oneness.

QUESTIONS

- When going on an adventure, do you know what your limit is?
- Do you have a "safety word" to let your partner know the limit has been reached?
- Do you give yourself the freedom to choose whatever you like to choose without justification towards yourself and others?
- Do you try to look at difficulties and tough situations you or others are in from a different perspective and from various sides?
- Do you have an inner connection and inner belief that you are supported by a higher power, whatever this means to you?
- Have you experienced a situation in which time felt like it stood still, with no thoughts or worries - only space, freedom, and bliss?
- Have you ever experienced unstoppable laughter?
- Are you ready to let bliss be a part of your life?

Lifehack: To gain an overview of any situation, look down from above so you can see the whole picture.

Isn't it fascinating to imagine all the huge colorful kites of kite surfers dancing in the air? It's incredible to see the mechanics of how the wind fills up the kites and launches the surfers, with boards strapped to their feet, across the water and the air. But it starts by learning to first maneuver yourself into a wetsuit. Can you feel and hear the powerful wind?

KITESURFING

She follows her intuition whenever she is inspired by the things she sees in magazines or hears people talk about. If it sparks her interest, nothing will stop her from finding out more about it. Where and how to learn it, what is required from her, and what are the risks involved, especial for beginners. She finds a five-day course up in the mountain close to St. Moritz, Switzerland, on the lake of Silvaplana, where they offer a kitesurfing camp along with accommodation. She enrolls herself and her hubby two weeks before the actual event. There is no time to prepare or improve her physical state, strength or flexibility before the course begins. When they arrive, it becomes clear that it's a man's world. Most of the participants of this kitesurfing camp are much younger than she is, and there is only one other woman, who works in the army and is used to physical workouts. What a discouraging and shocking start for her. The same situation often shows up in her life. She is the only beginner in the class, and as if that isn't enough, other than her hubby, is by far the oldest in the group. She has a choice. She can decide to play the victim, or she can embrace it. She chooses to see that the Universe has been gracious to her by affording her all the years she has had up until now. She hears herself say, *You wanted it, now you have it!* First, the instructor introduces them to the sport by teaching them various safety rules and skills in a meadow. How to properly manage the equipment, set up the kite, and control the kite once it's in the air. It's an exciting step: she feels the power of the wind when her kite is in the right position. To constantly look up at the kite above her makes her neck muscles tense. She feels as though her neck is lengthened like a giraffe's on her first flight. Compared to a child's kite, the dimension and force of this kite's power are astonishing. The next day, they meet at the kite center to get the wetsuits and neoprene booties. Back in the changing room she struggles to get into the tight wetsuit. Even this must be learned and practiced. She is both excited and nervous, not knowing whether she will be able to repeat the maneuvers she learned on land in the lake. It's time for the body drag in the water. She puts on the helmet and is assisted by her hubby who is also her kite buddy. As her buddy, he oversees helping her get in and out of the water, and to launch and land the kite. She carefully steps into the water and holds onto the kite, which has already been launched and connected to her harness and the bar she is holding onto. The lines of the kite are thirty meters long, which means she must be far enough out in the water and away from shore to make sure that if the kite drops down, it doesn't fall on a pedestrian walking along the shoreline. The feeling of being dragged behind the kite by sheer wind power is outstanding. A real adventure. Then it happens. She makes one wrong maneuver, and the kite drops down to the water surface. She tries with all her muscle power to get the kite up into the air again but has no luck. The kite pulls her closer and closer towards a bridge. Her hubby runs along the shore, jumps into the lake, and helps her to control the kite and get it out of the water. It becomes clear why they use a buddy system, especially for beginners. She is more than happy to have a hero as a spouse. In the evening, while they lie in bed, with all their muscles hurting after an exciting and physically exhausting day, they only have one wish: that there is no wind tomorrow! *Your wish is my command*, says the Universe. There is no wind the next day. They can now only imagine how they would lie in the water, putting their feet in the bindings on the board, positioning the kite so the wind will catch it and take them out of the water, letting them glide over the lake. Sometimes, only having a glimpse of something is enough of a gift.

QUESTIONS

- What are some of your interests that, just by thinking about them, release a huge amount of positive energy?
- What lights up your fire and excites you?
- How do you seek more information to expand your universe, online or in real life?
- Are there some similar situations you have found yourself in, which are more or less always challenging for you?
- Can you give yourself credit for the times you have practiced before performing?
- *Your wish is my command!* What wishes or commands do you have for the Universe for your personal life?

Have you ever traveled to a specific destination to do a certain sport? Your whole vacation was planned out, ensuring you got the experience you were hoping for, but then everything went in a different direction. So, you come to realize that you are better off accepting the situation and making the best of it, finding yourself being challenged, but also lucky. Instead of your actual plan, something else showed up which was just as interesting and fascinating to you. This happened to her too.

YOGA PART 1

The first interaction with yoga took place at the Gulf of Suez in Egypt. It is out in the middle of nowhere at a kite and wind surfing camp known for its wind stability. It is a challenge for her and her hubby to stay in such a rudimentary guesthouse, with an unspectacular meeting hall and a restaurant with plastic chairs and very basic food choices. There is nothing to do besides lie in the sun or shade, read a book and have the occasional swim in the sea, waiting and hoping that some wind will build up. They try to make the best of it by relaxing and surrendering to the situation, trying not to accomplish the common prejudice which hangs over watersport people. It brings her joy to chat to a woman who is a caregiver for animal actors and is in charge of the well-being of the animals when they are on the movie sets. Her clients are dogs, llamas or whatever is required in a certain movie. Their perception changes as they start to see their holiday as a vision quest. A yoga teacher from England is offering some hatha yoga lessons. Both haven't done it before. The first question for her is, what to wear? It won't be some fancy yoga wear, but rather shorts and a tank top, clothes which they already brought with them for the kite week. It's hot outside and inside, too. At least there are some fans in the yoga room. They are joined by other guests who have experience with the yoga exercises. She and her hubby can hardly do any of the asanas, trying to hold a pose, but losing their balance. The teacher cheers them on to give it a try. It is fantastic to be encouraged but not pushed too far, both feeling great and ready for another session the next day. The yoga instructor, who lives seasonally in this small resort, comes up with an original idea. A shopping experience for the two ladies on their own. They order a taxi and drive for thirty minutes to reach a tiny desert village, where they can count the number of houses with their fingers. She didn't know what she was saying yes to, but the opportunity to have an experience outside of the camp sounded very appealing. The yoga teacher walks determinedly towards a house which is actually a shop. In front of the shop is a clothes horse racked with items waiting to be chosen. Inside are more clothes, lingerie and bras, all presented on hangers. She is irritated that two male Arabic vendors sell bras and underpants to females. The yoga teacher is familiar with this situation and is very relaxed while trying on different pieces. *Oh làlà,* she thinks, as the yoga teacher selects some sexy underwear. She buys a long fashionable jeans skirt. It is a surprise to find those treasures in a place where only a gas station and a small shop with vegetables, fruits and daily household items exist. The two women feel like queens, merrily shopping and swinging their bags joyfully in the air, and this all out in the desert of Egypt! What a blast. What an amusing and harmless adventure, and a great story they get to share when they get back to their camp.

QUESTIONS

- What is your usual response if your expectations aren't met?
- Are you willing and able to decide to just make the best of it?
- Are you open enough to surrender the outcome?
- Which unsatisfying or difficult situations come to your mind where you found a way out of it by creating a good experience in the end?
- When was it that you found yourself being challenged but fortunate at the same time?
- What are some of the precious moments in these experiences where you felt like you had found treasures, and everything fell into place?
- What sparks feelings of joy in your life?

Imagine you decide to attend a hot yoga class. The room is heated up and you already feel warm outside. How will your body react and how will you calm your mind enough to surrender to the situation? Have some water and start to move your body, the temple of your soul.

YOGA PART 2

She loves doing physical bodywork. Why not try hot yoga? She has heard about it: there is always the same precise sequence of twenty-six postures and two breathing exercises which will be performed within ninety minutes in a heated room to allow the body to stretch, detoxify, relieve stress, tone, and heal chronic pain such as arthritis, joint aches, knee injuries, back problems, and more. She worries about her lower back because she often has pain and fells restricted by it, but her approach to new things is: Either don't try it at all, or dive in fully. While preparing at home, she considers wearing a t-shirt with long sleeves and long pants. She quickly changes her mind when she reads about what room temperatures will be awaiting her in the Bikram yoga studio. The room will be forty degrees Celsius with forty percent humidity! She starts to sweat at the thought of it. Her system feels much more comfortable around twenty-degree room temperatures. She hears herself say: *When you don't give yourself a chance to "get out of your daily comfort zone", you will never know what you could be experiencing! You might even gain huge benefits.*

She heard that the instructors won't demonstrate the moves, instead they are trained to talk the participants through the flow, as part of a moving meditation. Because she must listen to these cues, she will be forced to stop thinking and rather be in the moment. No matter where in the world someone practices Bikram yoga, the dialogue between the teacher and the student stays the same. It's time for her to step into the yoga center, get changed, put on short pants and a sleeveless top, all the while letting go of her concerns about her cellulite. She is not a zero-size model, nor an athlete. Most of the students are well toned. There's a professional swimmer with broad shoulders right next to her and on the other side of her mat is a very sexy handsome guy. It is a huge task to focus only on herself in the mirror in front of her and not get distracted by those well-trained bodies. She rakes around with her arms, trying to keep the balance. How beautiful it is to give herself a smile in those moments and receive a goodwill grin from the others. She knows everyone here started out in a similar way and increased their skills, flexibility, and muscle power over time. Shortly after the class starts, the heat of the room ruthlessly takes her fresh look away. She looks like she has taken a shower. Like a wet cat. Sweat is running down her face, her wet hair is sticking to her head, and her skin is shining. Not because of a luxurious body lotion, but because all her pores are unstoppable, releasing water in the form of sweat. So much discomfort. Advertisements show us how to prevent sweating, and that if you are a woman, it's only acceptable to sweat in a sauna. Now the secret is out: it becomes obvious why nearly everyone in the room is wearing a swimsuit, a bikini, or swimming trunks. It is great learning about body positivity and self-acceptance.

She remembers a sentence she read before the class.... When you start to feel uncomfortable, your gut instinct may be to drink water, wipe sweat, gulp in air, panic, look around, and then run from the room. How did the author of this article know precisely how she would feel in this studio? Luckily, another insight popped into her mind: If you feel dizzy, sit down and focus on trying to override the discomfort by using your breath. Trust that you can recover in less than one minute by simply closing your mouth and breathing through your nose. She is desperately looking forward to the Savasana, known as the corpse pose, or dead body pose. She lies flat on her back, chin slightly down to flatten the neck, her heels touching each other, feet open to keep her hips in alignment, and she puts her palms up. Lying there without moving, her eyes fully open, she is aware of her breath and practices letting go of any distractions. This pose calms her body, allowing her to soak in all the hard work that she completed in the first part of the class. She can sense her heart rate slowing down, her stress is relieved, and her body starts preparing for the second half of the class. She enjoys taking in the entire experience, even if it means not being able to move a single muscle without pain and stiffness the next day. What a blessing to have finished the whole ninety minutes. She got to know her body a little better, with a healthier approach towards herself and what her body can do. A big step towards self-love and self-appreciation.

QUESTIONS

- How well do you know your body?
- Do you feel energized and healthy? What could you do to improve your energy levels?
- How do you take care of your body?
- What else would be a great contribution towards your health?
- What do you like to implement daily to improve your well-being?
- How is your body image?
- What ability does your body have that you love?
- What body parts are you in love with?
- What are some body parts which need more kindness and gratitude from you?
- What brings a sparkle of joy to your body and soul?

Imagine how it would feel to laugh out loud and not hold your hand in front of your mouth, or feel shy or ashamed, and instead expose your teeth with a smile? A smile from the heart and from the belly, wonderful and freeing. Give love to every cell of your body by giggling so that dopamine will be activated. Welcome to the wellbeing of your soul and your body. Have a sneak peek at laughter yoga.

YOGA PART 3

She loves to laugh. Often, she gets recognized by her laughter. This is not because she only experiences joyful and happy moments in her life. Sometimes the laughter is forgotten. But the humor will show up again, and with it, the laughter. She hears about laughter yoga, and she knows laughter yoga is not a comedy. It is an exercise program for health and wellbeing. The yoga part of laughter is the combination of laughter exercises with yoga breathing techniques. Around the world, 110 countries have social laughter clubs. Laughter yoga is also being practiced in senior centers, schools and colleges, companies, corporations, factories, police stations and prisons. Nowadays it's very common to officially employ clowns in children's hospitals. Laughter as the cure. What an underestimated tool which is not often used in such a way in daily life. Laughter yoga is both preventive and therapeutic. She read that laughter releases endorphins which are natural pain killers that can help those suffering from arthritis, chronic migraines and headaches, chronic pains, autoimmune and chronic inflammatory diseases. It unwinds the negative effects of stress and strengthens the immune system. Laughter increases oxygen to the body and brain; this helps people to become energized. She decides to attend a one-day laughter workshop. It's one thing to read about something, and another to dive in and be confronted with your own limiting belief system and opinion on how a grown up should act, and what is strange or even immature. At the beginning, she and all the other participants are overstrained by trying to overcome the fear of looking foolish and being silly. Making awkward grimaces, noises and movements is like opening a treasure chest to sides of her personality she has never allowed herself to experience or allowed others to see, at least not since becoming an adult. It's so much easier to watch others be witty and playful than it is to put herself in the spotlight and not hold back ridiculous laughter or odd gestures, surrendering the outcome by just being amusing and present. The instructor explains a phenomenon to the group: adults tend to laugh from the mind and use judgments and evaluations about what's funny and what isn't. Children, who laugh much more frequently than adults, laugh from the body. After a good warm up and feeling more comfortable, the instructor goes on with several exercises. The silent laughter: opening the mouth wide and laugh without making a sound. Looking into each other's eyes. The greeting laughter: she walks around to different people with her palms pressed together near her upper chest in the Namaste greeting, and laughs. She and the other group members start by smiling and then slowly begin to laugh with a gentle chuckle, followed by a gradual increase in the intensity of the laugh until they have all achieved a hearty laugh. Gradually, everyone brings the laugh down to a smile again. After several hours of laughter, she can hardly smile anymore because her face muscles are so tired. It's like having completed a marathon; the body is exhausted, and the soul is filled with joy and dopamine, the happiness hormone. The workshop ends with everyone lying with their backs on the floor, in a circle, head-to-head next to each other so they can relax. In the middle of the calmness, someone suddenly starts giggling. It gets to the point where their body is shaking, and everyone joins in; no one can hold back anymore. The laughter is so intense it brings tears to her eyes. If she and the others hadn't gotten up from the floor to finish the workshop, they would still be lying there, holding their belly's, laughing until they had run out of tears. We all have a child inside of us who wants to freely laugh, play, and hum for fun and enjoyment.

QUESTIONS

- What have you defined as childish or not appropriate for you as an adult?
- How about laughing and giggling, do you let go and have outbursts?
- Are you comfortable making grimaces, using your face to express a greater extension of communication?
- What do like to laugh about?
- Are you able to laugh at yourself?
- Where can you bring more playfulness into your life, to nourish your whole system?
- What pops up right now?
- Are you open to invite and inhale more joyous moments in your life?
- Which movies do you like to watch because they are amusing, smart and fun? Make a list. Watch them again!

What is it that makes people travel around the world? What is your intention when you choose a country you would like to visit? Is it the nature, the people who live there, or are there other reasons? To include and appreciate the locals is an important part of my travels. Visiting different countries helps to loosen up our fixed point of views, gaining a wider perspective on how life can be lived.

BALI PART 1 - ROUNDTRIP

Most people dream about visiting Bali. She is lucky enough to experience the mist of this green plant island.

The humidity is very high. She looks like she has taken a shower and it's a wet-hair day. She couldn't care less about her hairstyle, make-up or her outfit. It's more about not fainting away.

She and her hubby are fortunate enough to have their own private driver and a guide who speaks English to drive them around the island and show them all the special spots and the mind-blowing scenery.

Because of the heat and the humidity, she feels as though she is drunk. She can't wait to get back to the car, to inhale the cold air from the air-conditioner. It's the same scenario every time they sit down on the backseat. They look at each other, with their half-closed eyes, begging to have a quick nap. Her hubby isn't any better off; both are totally exhausted by doing nothing but trying to survive the unfamiliar climate. It's a real dilemma they find themselves in. She traveled so far to see and experience Bali with all her senses, and now she only has one crazy wish, and that is to sleep.

They start to make a joke out of the situation. It's like a challenge: who is able to only grin but not laugh. That's quite a difficult task. As silly as it sounds, this helps them overcome the severe longing to sleep. When nothing else works, humor is often a really good solution and being that playful always, by magic, energizes them.

It's so wonderful to look out of the window of the car and take in the outrageous beauty on show while they travel to the next destination. It would be true to say that the journey is the real destination.

There are wild plants and people on their motorbikes everywhere. You would think that motorbikes have one or two people on them. Not in Bali. An entire family is seen holding onto each other on these bikes. The women are often dressed up very nicely, in shiny colorful long dresses, wearing sandals and flowers in their hair. The Balinese transport almost everything on their motorbikes. For her, the traffic rules are not clear; it looks as if there aren't any, but everyone else seems to navigate the crowded streets and all the chaos very well.

They witness a festive funeral procedure which is taking place on the side of the road. Life and death are so close together here and are not hidden behind walls. Every culture has their own way of celebrating and grieving. It's a gift to be amidst the Balinese daily life.

They pass by places where there are only huts made from clay, with people sitting in front of them, preparing something to eat. She sees no harshness or sadness in their faces, only happiness, gratitude, peace. Less is more.

She reflects on how being in the now probably looks like this.

The landscape is so rich, and the waterfalls are fascinating.

After having visited one of those waterfalls, they walk back on a narrow path towards the car. A beggar stands in their way and others join him. Everyone asks for money or attempts to sell art crafts to them. She feels captured in this uncomfortable situation. She doesn't wish to buy anything. She is confronted with the reality of people who almost don't have enough to live on. What role does the government have to play in this, how much do they care about their citizens?

In her life, she and her hubby also had to work for their money to afford a trip like this. They are contributing to the island and the people by booking hotels and guesthouses, eating out, having spa treatments, hiring a driver and a guide and so much more.

It's burdensome for her to recognize that some sort of envy is felt towards her from the people back at home who aren't able to take a vacation right now or have decided to spend their money on something else. On the other hand, she also feels how the responsibility of the well-being for the residents of holiday destinations, such as the Balinese, is put on tourists like them. She's never experienced this kind of overwhelming expectation before. She is assuming, because of their reaction, that they believe there should be dollar notes coming out of every pore of her body. She feels like a money machine. How can she develop and keep healthy boundaries towards the needs of others? They make their own sometimes difficult decisions but that is life. It is not only a difficult conversation during vacations but also in her daily lives. She knows she must work on it.

Every facet of life is reflected in the Balinese culture.

After this intense experience, they get into the car and visit the different kinds of temples, Puras, the expression of the Hindu religion. There are more than 20,000 of them. Seeing just a few of them is already time consuming, but they are truly mesmerizing.

She has the opportunity to have a quick peek out of the car window towards the amazing and beautiful rice terraces, in all the different shades of greens, which they plan to explore by foot on another day.

This private tour is interesting and inspiring; there is so much to see and learn.

Travelling around an island is very eye opening. There isn't only one way to live, one way to think or one way to act. Every culture has its own uniqueness.

While digesting what she sees in front of her eyes, and what she has taken in, she asks herself: Does she practice enough gratitude for what she has in her life, and does she nourish her inner self and mind with empowering thoughts?

QUESTIONS

- What countries have you visited?
- What are some of the nuggets you took out of every country?
- Are you able to include humor as a helping aid in a challenging situation?
- Are you open to trying it?
- What are healthy boundaries to you?
- Where do you have them already?
- Where do you feel it's necessary to apply healthier boundaries now?
- Where do you have to be clearer in communicating your boundaries?
- Where do you have to be unmistakable in terms of your actions for healthier boundaries?
- Are you able to try to not control others and their decisions, or do you feel responsible for them, even though it's not your duty?

Cooking, or more specifically, learning how to cook new and unfamiliar dishes, opens up a spectrum of experiences- new taste explosions and new ways of nourishing our bodies. To get to know, touch and cut new fruits and vegetables, and to cook with unfamiliar ingredients, is a feast for our eyes, nose, and palates; it's an expansion of our limitations. A plate of possibilities is served, and our bodies rejoice.

BALI PART 2 - COOKING LESSON

She decides to take a Balinese cooking lesson at a Balinese restaurant.

Early in the morning when the birds start to sing, she and her hubby get picked up in a small bus by the chef of the cooking class and one of his employees. They head straight to the market to get all the food they need for the cooking lesson and restaurant that evening.

As soon as they arrive at the food market, she has to put a tissue in front of her mouth because the overwhelming smell is too much for her. Her senses are so well developed. There is a potent smell of fish, too early in the day, and it confronts her stomach. Luckily, they are there to shop for vegetables and fruits too, which means they will move to another area of the market and away from the acrid smell.

When they arrive at the spot where the cooking lesson will take place, she is astonished at how like a sanctuary the place is. It is surrounded by green leafy plants and there are colorful flowers all over. The restaurant is without walls and is covered only by a bamboo roof to keep the guests dry from rain and protect them from the tropical sunshine.

The kitchen is located near the side of the restaurant. It's a small open building, with only a rooftop, one solid full-height wall, and a large stove and oven in front of it. The sides are open, so the air can circulate through the kitchen. There is a sink and some stone surfaces for food preparation, a kind of *mise en place*, as the French would call it.

It is a small class. Eight students from all over the world will try to create a special paste and some variants that will be used as the base of every main dish.

After the introduction by the head chef, they split into one-on-one groups, each equipped with a cooking apron, the recipe, a scale, and spoons of every size that will be used to measure the different herbs that must be combined to create those bases. The pastes from the students will be mixed with different kinds of fish, meat and vegetables. After the ingredients have marinated for several hours, they will be used for the evening meals which will be served to the guests of the restaurant, who have come to enjoy the delicious varieties of Balinese food.

Using the stove is quite a challenge for her because she has no desire to have the additional heat suffocate her. But it's a privilege to be together with this famous chef who has worked in other well-known hotels around the world. It's a recipe of feelings; having to concentrate on getting quality results while trying to have a fun, sensual experience with all those new spices.

She and her hubby are on one team, reading, measuring, and cooking. Usually they don't cook together, but why not give it a try. They're in Bali, after all.

Everyone is giving their best, wholly occupied in the process of creation.

The smell of all the ingredients is very satisfying, especially when they're sautéed and roasted. Coriander seeds, cumin, laos, kemirinut, shallots, garlic, crab paste, soya sauce, lime, kaffir lime leaves, chili, along with an array of spices she's never seen before, cooking together, filling the air with transcendental flavors and fragrances.

It's a pilgrimage, from the rustic noisy market with its salts of the earth to the lessons about Balinese food, and finally, Mecca: cooking and savoring it all. This is sacred.

It's time to take off the cooking apron and sit down and enjoy what the group has created this morning.

It's a small feast at lunchtime, with some chatting and laughter between the testing of different dishes, salads, and fruits. It's a stimulating gathering with foreigners, even more so now that they're all team members. To create something together can be such a wonderful and satisfying experience. Dinner is included in the package, but the chef recommends to all of his students that they book the dinner for another day. Rather come on an empty stomach so you can relish in the different kinds of food and enjoy the atmosphere of all the candles which adorn the garden. Dining with flower decorations on the tables and decent music in the background will afford them an entirely different experience. As a welcome gift, every guest gets a pink orchid to put in their hair.

It is blissful to be treated like a queen and king in the land of hospitality.

She knows, she will remember, even years from now, in places far from this, by the smell and the appearance of certain foods, what wonderful experiences she had in countries like Bali, where the food originally comes from.

To be connected to and able to use all your senses is such a gift. They can transport you all over the world.

QUESTIONS

- What food do you find delightful to smell and taste?
- Which dishes make your body rejoice?
- What food nourishes your body well?
- How can you enrich your meals? Why not use different spices and herbs to enhance the flavors?
- What about trying to cook a dish from a different culture?
- How about celebrating a meal and decorating the table nicely on an ordinary day? Life should be celebrated every day.

Lifehack: If you celebrate life, you nourish your soul.

Why not visit a spa, a time for the body and the soul? Get a treatment and allow yourself to be eased into a meditative state, a receiving state. All the senses are activated and in alignment, gifting your body with attention in a loving and caring way. Take the time to relax and recover. No effort is needed from your side. Just release what you are holding onto.

BALI PART 3 - SPA

She has made a reservation for a Lulur treatment at a spa in Ubud.

To get there, she must walk through a sacred monkey forest sanctuary. The monkeys are quite wily. Whenever they see a chance to grab something from the tourists, they do so. If it's a banana, a bag, a camera, or anything else they can carry, they will try, hoping to find something to eat. She walks hurriedly through the forest because she isn't that comfortable with the clinging monkeys.

She is relieved to arrive at the spa. This place was recommended by a friend of hers, who has been here before.

The Lulur treatment includes a body scrub, a body wrap, and finishes off with a bath.

She is introduced to one of the spa employees at the reception. She feels comfortable with this friendly young Balinese spa woman.

It's not a very fancy spa, rather a more traditional one. The walls are decorated with tiles and plants, and the wellness cabins are rather elementary but clean with an open roof.

First, she receives an exfoliating scrub which is made from natural ingredients like rice, turmeric, ginger, pandan and essential oils. The therapist gently applies the paste onto her entire body, leaves it to dry, and then scrubs it off, eliminating dead skin cells with it. While the spa employee performs her work with finesse, they talk about the Balinese culture, women in her society, daily life, and vice versa. There is power in spaces where women trust each other. She rinses off under a warm shower and readies herself for the next step: the body wrap. One yogurt body wrap is applied, followed by another. During the course of the treatment, she can hear the birds singing and Balinese music playing in the background.

A bathtub filled with wonderful flowers and essential oils to soak in awaits her. This will complete the Lulur experience. She will be reborn. She slides into the lukewarm water, and all the different flowers in all colors float around her and flatter her body. She feels like a princess. Not feeling judged is so freeing. For the Balinese women, a woman with curves is very attractive. Where she comes from, a lot of women try to be slim to feel desirable. To lie in this flower bath, losing sense of time and worries, is spiritual. Healing. Being taken care of in such an appreciative way helps leave the fear and anxiety behind. Floating in the moment.

A lovely tea is served. With each sip she is transported into a bath of love and self-acceptance.

QUESTIONS

- What are some recurring sentences which you hear yourself saying to your body?
- How do you judge and shame your body?
- Are you committed to changing your thoughts surrounding your body from blaming to adoring? What would this sound like? Write it down.
- Do you give your body credit for being such a powerful contribution to your life?
- Do you try to fit into the norm, or are you more or less at peace with how you look?

Lifehack: Create a praise ritual for you and your body.

Rice is a precious and good commodity eaten all around the world. It is used as a main course, a side dish, or as a dessert. You may choose different kinds of rice, depending on where you are in the world. It is marvelous to see how and where it grows in the beautiful rice terrasses of Bali. It's a real privilege and a unique experience to be that close to the rice farmers and the rice field guide. What about being one of the few foreigners invited to attend the festival?

BALI PART 4 - RICE FIELD AND FESTIVAL

Arriving at a cozy guesthouse next to a rice terrace feels like home to her. There are different huts located in an area like the garden of Eden. Greenery and flowers everywhere. Even a little swimming pool is hidden below the main building. All the staff are friendly and debonair towards her and her hubby.

There is an altar by a small wall at the entrance. It's called Canang sari and it's a bowl made out of palm tree leaves decorated with flowers, oils, salt, and some rice.

She first noticed them when they took a trip around Bali. There are offerings all over the floor, on the walls or in the shrines.

Balinese people are peaceful. They always try to be in harmony with their gods. They have two ways of living in harmony: Ask the good for assistance and appease the evil. For this reason, the offerings are located at all possible points of conflict, such as crossroads or bridges, the front of shops, houses, cars, hotels, temples, on the beach, and her bungalow too.

Their bungalow has a triangular bamboo rooftop, a spacious room with a bed and a mosquito net. Above it all hangs a fan, and there are windows with a fantastic view of the rice terraces. They spotted a bigger family friend of the lizard called a gecko on the wall. This will be their local pet for the duration of their stay. It's good for her and her hubby, as they know the gecko will eliminate the mosquitos.

Early the next morning, they wait to get picked up by a personal rice terrace guide.

Most of nature is still asleep at this time. The sun starts to rise, and the early morning mist still hangs over the fields, which makes it very mystical.

While she and her hubby walk along the wonderful luscious intense green paddies, they enjoy listening to the guide who shares his knowledge of agriculture and his own culture. Every rice field has a unique aspect. They are all gorgeous in their own way. The Balinese community views rice as a gift from God and a symbol of life. For thousands of years, the Balinese people have been growing rice and cultivating the beautiful rice terraces of Bali where three kinds of rice are grown: white rice, black rice, and red rice. What makes the Balinese rice terraces so unique is the Subak irrigation system which even made it into the UNESCO World Heritage Sites list. The Subak system is a manifestation of the Tri Hita Karana philosophy that is part of Balinese culture. Tri Hita Karana consists of three principals:

Harmony among people, Harmony with nature or the environment, and Harmony with God.

It's so peaceful to be out in this magnificent and beautiful nature with no one else in sight.

After the tour, he invites them to his own guesthouse to have some breakfast.

They aren't used to being invited to strangers' homes. They don't really know what to give in return or what is expected from them, but she hears herself say: *Just go with the flow.*

While sitting on the terrace, taking in his hospitality, enjoying a delicious breakfast made of black rice which is served on a banana leaf, they have some quality time with other guests and the friendly Balinese guide. He mentions that there is a special feast taking place in the village later that same evening. He invites them to join him and offers to pick them up at their guesthouse. They take the chance to expand their universe.

Back at their Bungalow, the guide informs the employees and asks them if they could help her and her hubby find something suitable to wear.

The whole staff gathers around the couple and assists them in putting on the special clothes. They giggle and have so much fun seeing her in a knitted sage colored blouse which is certainly not made for a European-sized woman. Thank God the material is somewhat elastic, so she can wear it. He will wear an Udeng on his head. It suits him well. Both are wearing a sarong as a bottom.

In the evening they are collected by their guide, as promised. The staff wishes them well. It's a special honor to be a guest with a few other foreigners. Canang sari and Gamelan music fill the air all around them.

To bear witness to this moment and be included in such a significant religious festival, so important to everyone attending the event, is so touching. She has tears in her eyes as she sits on the floor and realizes how she has been welcomed by everyone, no exclusion, and no judgment. With gratitude, she receives what the Universe has offered to her.

QUESTIONS

- What goods and qualities do you not want to miss in your life?
- Foodwise?
- Lifestyle wise?
- Nature or environment wise?
- Relationship wise?
- Social life?
- How important is it for you to have harmony in your life?
- With whom do you have the desire to be in harmony and have a great exchange?

Do you ever think about learning a new sport? I believe it's always fun to experience something new, even if thinking about it makes you a little scared. Sometimes feeling a bit scared about something new is not feeling scared at all - it's actually excitement! Are you content with your life as it is, or looking forward to learning something new? Do you avoid this because it's a challenge? Have you ever considered laughing about an uncomfortable situation or using humor to ease the tension?

LEARN TO SCUBA DIVE PART 1

She has always been drawn to being involved with the various elements of nature. She loves water in particular because it makes her feel free. She feels connected to it in a way. This could be because the human body comprises 70 percent water.

The earth is a watery place, in both liquid and frozen forms. About 75 percent of the earth's surface is water-and the oceans hold about 96.5 percent of all the earth's water. Water also exists in the air in the form of vapor, in rivers and lakes, in icecaps and glaciers, in the ground as soil moisture and in aquifers and plants.

Water is an essential elixir. It is precious on its own and in combination with other elements. It's a playground, a companion, a healer, a transportation tool, an instrument, and an entire universe for so many animals and plants and more.

She has already learned one of the water activities, swimming. This summer she and her hubby decide to not only swim on the surface of the water but dive under it as well. Scuba diving, while extreme, is also very tranquil. They booked the PADI Open Water Dive Course at a lake close by. First, they learn all the theory about diving, and the purpose of all the equipment which will be used. They then do some practical preparation on how to correctly put the equipment together. Things like the regulator, depth gauge, submersible pressure gauge, the dive computer, and the buoyancy compensator. After the beginner's session is complete, she heads to the bathroom to jump into her neoprene-smelling wetsuit and boots. She swings her dive belt with the weights onto her hips. Her nervousness increases while fastening the belt. Lastly, the neoprene hood comes on. A feeling of claustrophobia comes up. She senses the tension build up in her whole body. The hood is an advantage, because the water temperature of the lake isn't that high, and the hood will do its job to maintain her body temperature and prevent her from freezing. She puts on the buoyancy compensator jacket as well as the heavy Scuba tank which is attached to it and all the other gear she'll need. It feels like carrying a heavy sack of potatoes around on her back. She feels like a bizarrely decorated Christmas tree. Awareness is a safety requirement when wearing and walking with unfamiliar gear. Even the short distance along the promenade to the pier is risky. Glancing around makes her feel like she is a space explorer from another planet. Her prancing around in this kit while everyone else is either sunbathing in their bikinis or making themselves comfortable on their cozy colorful sun blankets justifies the feeling. The sun is burning her head and body, and she feels like she is in a greenhouse. The sweat trickles down her forehead. After successfully putting on the fins, it's time to put on her mask and get ready to jump from the pier into the lake.

QUESTIONS

- Do you want to learn a new sport?
- What excites you about this sport?
- What are the doubts you have about learning this sport?
- What is your biggest apprehension and fear?
- Does your mindset limit you?
- What adaptions do you have to make before you are actually willing to do it?
- How can you experience this sport without a lot of effort? Is there a way for you to have a trial?
- How much longer are you going to wait?

Have you ever experienced a scary situation where you wanted to quit what you were doing, or get out as quickly as possible? Already playing the movie out and seeing the devastating ending? Can you still control yourself, even if anxiety and panic arise? For me, this is a serious challenge, and I know I'm not broken if I decide to give up. There will be more opportunities to give it a try. Remember, you are not the only person who struggles with panic; there are millions of people around the world who do too. You are not broken just because some situations are triggering for you.

LEARN TO SCUBA DIVE PART 2

Standing on the pier, her eyes are wide open, and panic is written all over her face. She feels like she is unable to breathe. Her mask gets foggy, and not being able to see anything induces a panic attack. Her Scuba instructor is well experienced, and sees this all the time, students getting stressed out when putting their masks on, only to have them fog up. She has one thought on her mind, and that is to rip off the equipment immediately, leave, and never come back. She reaches the point where her heart rate is dangerously high. She nearly fades away and her whole body system heats up with tension. Her instructor quickly recognizes the signs and knows how to support her. He says, "I know you are not comfortable right now, but trust me, if you get into the water, you can clean the mask there, and if you go slightly under the water, you'll see again, cool down and you will be fine." The confidence, comfort, and stability he gives her in this moment gives her the courage not to quit. She looks down and takes the leap. Ahhhhh, what a relief to feel the cold water circulate in her wetsuit and especially around her head and face. She follows her instructor's advice on how to clean the mask, and to check if the regulator she has put into her mouth to breathe is working perfectly. The regulator makes it possible for her to breathe the air from her tank by converting the high-pressure air into ambient pressure.

She asks herself: *Am I really ready to dive?* The instructor knows how to ensure that she stays in the present and overcomes her fear. He indicates to her to stay close to the water's surface, while he takes her hubby a little further down. It helps to preoccupy her to watch him take her hubby deeper. He heads back up to the surface to take her a little further down while her spouse attempts to keep himself in place. Her hubby struggles to hold the position and starts floating towards the surface again. She sees this as an opportunity to quickly flee herself but before she can, the instructor grabs her hubby by his leg and pulls him back again. She is consciously entertained by her instructor so that there is no space for concerns and fear. After being underwater for a while, they go back up. Grabbing the metal ladder brings relief. They take off their fins and masks before climbing up the ladder to get on the pier again. How liberating, she has done it! She overcame her anxiety and now an entire underwater world awaited her and her hubby. After several more lessons, as well as working with a therapist on her fears and anxiety, claustrophobia and self-doubts, she passes the written and practical test and receives the PADI, the Open Water Diver Certification. The magical underwater world of the Maldives was now waiting for her.

QUESTIONS

- How much would your life change for the better if you decided to take action towards a dream of yours?
- Are you allowing yourself to succeed?
- Are you allowing yourself to be the first one in your family or circle of friends to experience it?
- Are you aware that you can send the fear and the doubts which don't belong to you back to sender?
- Do you understand that this new experience could fill you with pride and satisfaction?
- What else do you like to feel after overcoming a fear-related experience and challenge?
- What do you hope to get out of this sport or activity for your own personal life?

Do you have difficulty flying? Do you enjoy it, or have you experienced fear, anxiety or even panic attacks in the past? Perhaps you don't even consider flying because of your claustrophobia? She has been through ALL of it, by plane, train, and car. It not only happens while traveling but in her daily life too. There is no "one size fits all" solution, but she likes to share some helpful tools and techniques from her own experiences. One of the most encouraging thoughts in such a stressful situation is to breathe and say to yourself: *This won't last forever, this will pass.*

TO FLY AND SEE THE WORLD

To visit and see the world, YES please. But flying? One of the most stressful things for her is flying. Being trapped in a plane triggers her whole nervous system. She wants to escape this claustrophobic feeling as soon as possible- or even better, not have it in the first place. Her body creates an unbearable heat. She begins to sweat and gets overwhelmingly nervous to the point where her mind becomes foggy. Not the best way to start a vacation. But if she wants to travel some distance and explore new cultures, flying is often the best or only solution.

There are people who are afraid during take-off and others that are scared and have anxiety at the thought of landing. For her it's another scenario. The moment when all the doors of the airplane close, knowing she has to sit it out, unable to leave, is terrifying for her.

She knows she will be better off having an aisle seat. This gives her a feeling of more spaciousness and air around her, which is helpful for people with claustrophobia. It's also easier to walk around or go to the toilet.

She takes water along to help her when she gets overheated in those stressful situations. Water works the fastest to cool and calm her down. She makes sure to buy herself some water bottles after she passes the security check, so she doesn't have to wait for the flight attendant to offer her some. She carries some refreshing tissues with her as well. She uses functional, cooling fabrics which can be activated by watering and moving them around in the air to chill again.

Taking the responsibility of being prepared is a powerful and helpful tool for her.

In addition, she keeps a roll-on with a calming and refreshing essence in her bag. If needed, she applies it to her wrists, temples, neck, and belly. This helps her feel instantly more relieved and centered again.

Her shoes are important too. To regulate her body-heat balance, flip-flops or sandals are fine, they are easy to take off if required. She wears different layers of clothes which she can easily remove to make herself a little more comfortable.

She knows that for some people, flying is like watching a movie: a very relaxing experience. But for her it's different and that's ok too.

The most effective and supportive approach for her is to consider and ask herself ahead of time, what is the proportion between her fear and the possibilities and gains that will be generated out of this situation? Often the fear ranks the highest (5), and the gains are very low (1). Now it's on her to increase the possibilities up to 5 and decrease the fear down to 1 to create the anticipation and the excitement of the gain which is in front of her.

How does she actually do this? A magic wand? No. She asks herself the important question: What will I miss if I don't do it? It doesn't matter if its flying, diving, learning, or trying something new, if she allows it, these challenges will prevent her from exploring the treasures of life. Many people refuse to expose themselves to their fears or anxieties, and rather choose to play it safe, to surround themselves with the familiar and never challenge themselves, and that's ok too! Everyone may choose the life they want to experience.

QUESTIONS

- Are you ready to take full responsibility for your wellbeing?
- What are some methods and affirmations you use ahead of and during challenging situations?
- What tools do you use when you are in the middle of a stressful situation?
- Do you remember to breathe?
- Do you use possibilities and probability to assist you?
- Are you ready to ask this important question: What will I miss if I don't do it?
- Are you open to creating excitement with what you can gain?

Lifehack: Why don't you give it a try and thank yourself for confronting your fear or anxiety. Yes, it sounds peculiar, but it works.

Wow, 26 stories later, perhaps you have already discovered your personal SHE, or parts of her. If you now know and feel that you can't put the book down, I would like to hear how SHE looks in your life as you uncover more personal growth with each story. Let's have a look at how you can shine even brighter, with me at your side. I'm here for you.

www.sonja-shine.com

These QR codes will open the doors
to a wonderous universe for you.

A Shower Inspiration Meditation

The Shower Inspiration Meditation is a short, easy-to-use free meditation perfect for while taking a relaxing shower or sitting comfortably somewhere quiet, to enthuse you to find out more about your deepest dreams and desires and encourage you to put them on your heart list and explore them. SHINE!

My Facebook Group

My Facebook group is a sacred space for you to share the successes of your own Sonja Moments, your SHINE Moments; to share the challenges you have overcome and to connect with others who are also on their heart journeys. The group is for encouraging one another and is a way for you to find out about my offers and programs- and occasionally have a Zoom session to get to know your SHINE! community.

Prepare for your next adventure.

Unconditional love are two epic words, and they show up for everyone in a different way. Unconditional love in a love relationship between friends, in family relationships, and in the relationship towards yourself, is a tall task. It's the love you offer freely, without expecting anything in return. How does this generosity feel? How do you consciously receive it? Let's see what it is all about it and what her hubby offers her.

UNCONDITIONAL LOVE

She is ready to explore the world. The taxi is waiting to pick them up and drive them to the airport. With every passing kilometer, her adrenalin and anxiety increase. Is she open to receive it?

The worry about having to fly for ten hours to get to the Maldives and then taking a small water plane afterwards is hanging over her.

A long trip lies ahead of her but knowing that her hubby has offered her this unbelievable opportunity calms her down.

She feels so loved, heard, and seen, even in the uncertainty of how she will cope being locked up in an aircraft for such a long time.

Tears of gratitude and appreciation roll down her cheeks.

Whenever she feels stressed or feels like she has to turn around and go home, she finds comfort that this is an option, and she doesn't need to explain or justify herself to him. The option to change her mind is always there; forget about the ticket or the hotel, whether they're still in the airport before starting the trip, or when they land in Male. If she so chooses, they could take a plane straight back home. Even if they are already on the island and are enchanted by paradise, and she feels captured, there will always be the option to go home. What an enormous gift. It reveals the full impact and importance of the love they have for each other. How much do they really care for each other? She can't put into words what this means to her. Perhaps unconditional love describes it best.

With this wild card she feels as though an enormous weight has been lifted from her shoulders. She is more prepared to accept the challenge of flying and be open enough to receive what waits on the other side.

She knows how to take care of herself during the flight. With her self-help survival kit and the right mindset, and, of course, now with the wild card, anything is possible.

She enters last to avoid the long wait until the air conditioner starts and some cool air comes towards her.

A close friend gave her some helpful advice - just be the plane. You and the plane must melt together and the whole trip will be just like a trip in a train or on a bus. Of course, it's bumpy once in a while, but that's normal.

She tries this empowering secret from her friend and is more than amazed at how well it's working. Surprisingly, there are no more thoughts of leaving the plane.

It's so helpful to be able to ask for a practical tip or encouragement from a loved one or a professional. Some internal work has to be done by herself, and some energetic support will help too.

To ask for help and to be ready to receive it is the process of personal growth.

Thinking about this thoughtful gift which her husband has given to her gives her the confidence that she will experience the whole trip and the stay on the lovely island and will see it all as a wonderful present.

They arrive at Male and suddenly there isn't even a thought of considering flying home. Instead, she is curious about the small water airplanes which are waiting to bring the tourists to their final destination on one of the islands which are scattered all over the ocean.

She will connect with the small plane as she did with the bigger plane before. She increases her gratitude for the fact that she has the chance to see these impressive inventions.

His generosity is all-embracing. There is always a solution. A manageable way to solve a problem. He knows that she would happily do the same for him. That's one of the secrets of their long, loving marriage. Finding the balance between her and him as individuals and as a couple too.

QUESTIONS

- What does unconditional love mean to you?
- What does unconditional love look like in your relationship?
- What adaptions in your relationship would be beneficial for both of you?
- Where do you feel you could open your mind up even a little more towards your partner?
- What is the secret of the success of your love relationship?
- Where and when do you struggle to ask for help and support, or to fully receive it when it does come?
- Where and when is it easy for you to receive?
- Are you balanced in giving and receiving in all your different kinds of relationships: in your love relationship, with your children, with your parents, your siblings, relatives and your friends?

Lifehack: It's about a healthy balance in all relationships!

Have you ever noticed how small we are as humans? She notices this more than ever looking out of the window on the flight to the Maldives. We are the center of our own personal lives, but the truth is that we are also only one piece of a very large puzzle. To have the opportunity to fly high above with knowledge and insight of what lies below is phenomenal. What a creative invention. Are you ever astonished by the colors and structures of planet earth? Why don't you come along with me to explore all your different senses?

MALDIVES PART 1 - FIRST SIGHT

Is she dreaming? No, this is real. The Maldives are waiting to be admired. Flying over the vast ocean into the carefully placed islands overwhelms her. The colors are so intense: the blue sky, the different shades of blue of the ocean, the greens of the islands and all the different colors of the reefs. The inner artist in her rejoices in all the beauty. She hears her soul saying, *The universe is the biggest creator*. Getting out of the narrow and noisy water airplane is a relief, especially after the long airplane trip before. The breeze of fresh air and the sight of all the colored fish swimming beneath the pier fills her with joy. The sound of her flip-flops on the pier en route to the reception brings a smile to her face. They soon step off the end of the pier. It's time to be barefoot and one with the sand. It will be like this for the remainder of their stay. She appreciates the warm welcome from the staff, who provide gifts on arrival, which include some yummy coconut ice cream, lemon-infused water and a cooling towel to refresh herself. Here she is in paradise. The singing and drumming of the staff are also heartwarming.

To have everything she enjoys within easy walking distance is very convenient for her. She is staying in a sea bungalow which is set on wooden pillars. Small crabs cling onto the timber, various shaped and colored fish, turtles, and reef sharks come close to the beach. She loves the exclusivity of it all.

To have the choice to connect with others or enjoy the privacy on the wooden bungalow creates a more gratifying experience. Her bungalow is decorated with red fabrics which complement the romantic four-poster bed. She loves the effortless meditation that comes from staying in the present and observing the waves from the terrace.

She enjoys walking barefoot, feeling the fine sand moving between her toes while walking on the beach to the main building for meals. There's a choice between two paths, depending on the time of day. One has more shade, while the other is more exposed to the sun.

To be kissed by the sun and embraced by the wind is the perfect combination. She will occasionally walk into and under the water too. She feels so fortunate to be able take in the beauty of this island, surrounded by all its soft white sand, different shades of green, and the flowers that spread their perfume through the air. Everything is so indulgent. Having so much gratitude for all this magic, and feeling blessed, leaves her asking herself, *What more could I ask for*?

QUESTIONS

- What signifies paradise for you?
- When and where do you like to connect with others or rather prefer to enjoy privacy?
- Do you give yourself the choice of being social or isolated, depending on your needs?
- What do you have to do in order to have some privacy and time on your own?
- What actions do you need to take right now to achieve this?
- When last did you experience peace?
- What do you enjoy doing: watching the waves, being in the woods, or laying in the grass or something else?
- Where can you use nature as a meditation without much effort?
- What does your inner dialogue sound like?
- What kinds of feelings and emotions do you have in those moments of bliss?

Perhaps you have also been exploring your limits? Reading or watching a certain sport or activity is never the same as being in the middle of it and feeling the emotions that come with it. She gets centered again. Conscious breathing always brings her back into the moment. It helps her tremendously to know that her hubby is right there to help if need be. There is limited communication under water. The most important communication is the one with yourself. Do you let your mind run wild or can you control it, if necessary, say STOP? Because the worries of your mind are holding you back from your full potential. Healthy boundaries within your mind are fundamental both underwater and on the surface, in every facet of your life.

MALDIVES PART 2 - DIVE

She finds herself on a diving boat in the Maldives. She goes from her beloved safe island out to the open blue sea. The water is clear. Here and there she passes by shiny white sand bars and other beautiful small islands. She doesn't know if she will have the courage to take a dive into the open blue. The electric atmosphere created by this group of experienced divers who get ready to check their diving equipment is nearly too much for her.

As each minute goes by, the excitement arouses her body and mind. Even though her hubby is also a beginner, just knowing he is nearby brings her comfort. It's difficult for her to keep the concentration when she hears the briefing by the dive master. He explains what to expect with the current, and the special fish which are often found in this area. Spitting into the mask to prevent it from getting foggy isn't nearly as much of a challenge as zipping up the wetsuit is. It's tight and narrow, especially around the bust and the neck. The sound of the boat's engine disappears. It's now time to put on the fins, weight belt, and the Scuba tank which is attached to the life jacket. This includes the breathing regulator, the dive computer and the mask. She waits to be assisted by the boat crew; they make sure everything is fine and that she gets safely with the heavy equipment and her duck feet, the fins, to the edge of the boat to be all-clear to enter the ocean. The water is refreshing.

Breathe, breathe, breathe ... Everything is fine... she says to herself, holding the inflator to let all the air out of her jacket. She does this to allow herself to sink.

Instead of exhaling, she is so overwhelmed that she takes another long breath as if it were her last. It's all in her mind. This causes a delay for her. She still swims on the surface, while all the others descend deeper into the unknown. Afraid that the others have to wait for her, she feels like she is too late. She gives it another go, and is now underneath the water, and her mask sits perfectly. Her breath regulator is working, oxygen goes into her lungs, and she can hear herself breathe. She tries to slow and calm her breathing and gets close to her buddy. Everything seems ok. As she was informed, the steep dark wall shows up on her right-hand side; she has never seen such an impressive one before. The divers are behind each other and there is a current, not a strong one, but still strong enough to let her know she is not totally in control. She is taken aback by the dimension of the rock formation and caves chiseled into the wall. Excitement suddenly ignites inside her. The dive master dives into one of the caves and signals to the group to get away from the entrance, immediately. An enormous sea turtle who resides in there woke up and is swimming towards the group. Not having the proper skill to move backwards and out of her way takes a lot of her oxygen. Her bottle only has a certain amount of oxygen, and she is very concerned that she will use hers too quickly because of restlessness. If this should happen, her buddy and even perhaps the whole group might have their trip end prematurely. The pressure is mounting. How can she relax and enjoy the beauty if she burdens herself with this fear? At this moment, she remembers a friend who once said: People in a group are always happy to find out that there is someone else in the group with less experience, less skills, and less stamina than themselves. Her inner dialogue begins: *Don't wiggle your arms around, it burns too much energy and compromises your inner peace.* Some more turtles show up. Appreciation increases, for all those fascinating creatures of nature. Still in her own world, floating in this huge natural aquarium, she almost doesn't notice the dive master calling them over to have a look at something. She points her flashlight in the direction the dive master is calling them. Everybody is trying to get a look, the ones in back are pushing the ones in the front. She doesn't like this hassle at all. She decides to maneuver herself away from all the impatient divers. She is feeling trapped and lacked support from the experienced divers. All of that brings on a panic attack. She feels like throwing up, that she can no longer breathe, and nearly faints.

She feels her heart banging in her chest, anxiety is in all her cells. She feels like she must flee directly up to the surface as quickly as possible. Her thoughts are spinning, and then her inner voice tells her: *You are not allowed to go directly to the surface, you have to make a safety stop at five meters for three minutes. Why don't you calm yourself down, everything is fine, even though this situation is very uncomfortable. Don't show your buddy the state you are in right now, he will be overwhelmed. Better you try to sort this out on your own first.* She hears herself saying that if this unbearable situation goes on any longer then you may use your blackboard to write down, 'Help, I'm panicking and feel claustrophobic, I'm going up.' Her decision to ask for help if it gets worse immediately gives her access to a more self-empowering mindset. She deliberately keeps herself occupied by looking around, fascinated by the variety of fish and their colors, while trying to get her body into a more stabilized position. That instantly helps and she feels more in control. She still has enough oxygen to take additional breaths of excitement in. The shift of her inner dialogue and being a little more connected with her body gives her subconscious enough information to let her know not to worry and that everything is under control. This uncomfortable situation won't last forever. After talking calmly and supportively to herself, breathing consciously in and out, she gets into a space of trust and freedom. Now she is ready to show her buddy that she would like to hold hands with him, and that she needs his connection and vibes of relaxation. She feels so proud of herself. She knows now that she can count on herself. Back on the beach, without a diving mask in the way, she communicates her discomfort vulnerably and honestly. Yes, she will have to see a professional about the trauma, but for now, she feels gratitude and relief.

QUESTIONS

- Are you sometimes afraid you could be a burden to others?
- How well are you already connected to your body and soul?
- Do you hear and feel the needs your lovely body has?
- Do you support your body and your mind with good energetic thoughts and actions?
- How do you cope with unpredictable situations?
- Are there any situations that come to mind where you knew you could count on yourself and were more capable than you ever thought you might be?
- Are you open to look at a trauma that may prevent you from reaching your full potential?
- Are you ready to reach out for a professional to facilitate you?
- What would you like to share with your partner, that you have never shared with anyone else, because you know it's now time?

What a fun creation, to have boards in all shapes and for such a variety of different sports. The universe of boards consists of snowboards, which is what she is used to riding, but not kickboards, surfboards, and wakeboards, all with unique patterns and color combinations. It's all about finding your balance, which is a metaphor for life too. It's no secret that you will enter a new dimension and feel so satisfied when you find the flow. Having a direct connection to the elements in which you are moving is unmistakably liberating. It doesn't matter whether you have a board or not. Let's get on the board.

WAKEBOARDING

She finds it fascinating watching the wakeboarders on the lake. Splashing the pressurized water beneath their boards while holding a rope connected to the boat. Immense energy, not only for the boat but for the energy of the sportive approach and performance of the boarders too. They are even able to jump over the waves which are created by the boat. They use these waves to perform tricks with their boards. She is keen to try, so before she loses interest, she heads out towards the wakeboard center. Being on vacation helps her remain relaxed. Everyone is laidback and much younger than her, but no matter what, she is determined to give it a try. It is now or never. She wears a rash-guard long-sleeve shirt and Lycra leggings to protect herself. She slides into the water with her lifejacket, takes hold of the wakeboard handle and receives instructions on how to improve the board position to take off. She has to adjust herself into the starting position with every wave that comes her way. She doesn't rush, and instead takes the time she needs to get herself ready to take off. The engine of the boat is roaring. She hears herself shout to overrule the noise of the motor of the boat. *I'm ready, go!* She lets go of one hand to give a thumbs up. She can feel how powerful the boat is by the way it pulls her out of the water. She remembers not to straighten her legs too fast otherwise she will fall out in front. She succeeds! She stands and gets towed by the boat. Her hubby sits on the backseat of the boat and cheers. He is rejoicing seeing her alive and happy. She can feel her muscles getting weaker by the minute. She can't do any tricks, but to be on her feet and not in the water is already a victory. She is even able to look around. She notices some really enormous and elegant houses, almost palaces, along the beach. Her focus returns to her body again, and her muscles tell her they are not enjoying themselves anymore. Her legs are shaking because they have been active the entire time, and minute by minute her arms are finding it difficult to hold on.

She can feel the speed of the boat and the wind blowing into her face, and with it, how fast she wakes behind the boat. She could probably hang on a bit longer but chooses to let go of the wakeboard handle and sinks slowly into the ocean. She feels grateful to have experienced such an amazingly powerful sport activity.

QUESTIONS

- When did you first experience the power of your own sports performance?
- How did you feel?
- What was your mindset then?
- Do you like to get into contact with sports activities, and if so, which one?
- Do you use this momentum, or do you often hear yourself say, perhaps tomorrow or another day?
- What helps you prevent procrastination? What's your secret?
- What is your motivational catchphrase to get yourself going?

Lifehack: Now or never!

Have you ever wondered what it would be like to dive into a world of luxury and extravagance which isn't necessarily accessible to everyone, while not having to spend a fortune on it? Appreciating how life can unexpectedly bless you just by you being open enough to see the opportunity will do you a world of good. There is no need to wait until the universe presents you with a gift; instead, be curious and have respect towards other cultures. Go with the flow of life and expect good things to happen.

ARABIC WORLD PART 1 – DESERT RESORT

She found an offer to good to be true for their stay in a hotel resort out in the desert in the Arab Emirates. They arrive at the impressive airport of Dubai. Welcome to a world of success, opulence and shiny things.

They are collected by their driver. It's already dark when they arrive at the resort. A quick check-in followed by a hurried accompaniment to their room is all they're after. Outside all the exclusive bungalows are some lights which give the whole accommodation a very inviting atmosphere.

Their bungalow is divided into two sizable rooms. One is a bedroom, more like a living room, with a huge bed in it. It has an extravagant chandelier set in the ceiling above as well as a writing desk and a big sofa. Everything is of a high quality and standard. It's very impressive to her. She loves those carefully chosen fabrics. The other room is split up into two sections: one with the white exclusive bathtub which is situated in the middle of the room, and the other is a dressing room. There are blue and warm white lamps embedded into the floor. It looks like a private spa. From the bathtub she can see toward the dressing room, and there is an oversized round seat – a pouf, made from velvet, in a powdery rose shade that she can sit on or lay her clothes down on. She imagines how fun it would be to be alone with some Arabic women, enjoying a gathering, sitting on this furniture and sharing beauty tips, with tea and some delicious Arabic sweets by their side. For now, this is only a dream of hers. Beside the dressing room is a beautiful big shower which has enough space to dance in. For practical reasons as well as for creating an atmosphere, the walls and windows in the two rooms are all covered with white satin curtains. The whole bungalow and terrace as well as the pool and the small garden are surrounded by elegant walls so that every guest may have total privacy and a wonderful view towards the desert.

She feels like a queen and a goddess, over-indulging in luxury she would never be able to afford if it were not for the special she received.

To have this once-in-a-lifetime privilege is a gift from the Universe she intends to embrace.

In the morning, right after breakfast, she explores all the different buildings she was unable to see when they first arrived in the middle of the night. First, her husband escorts her to the reception.

This time, fully awake, she spots the huge vases filled with gorgeous flowers, and all the walls are adorned with dark wooden Arabic ornaments. Artful mosaics are set in the marble floor. She takes a peek into the spa area. Lovely inviting scents hover towards her. She knows she will have to make another stop here and enjoy the treatments.

There are two restaurants here. Food sorted. That's always good to know, especially when located out in the desert.

As if out of nowhere, she is pulled into a room which is located in the main building. She feels like she is in the wrong place, as if she has stepped into a private meeting. An Arabic family is seated inside, on a long, colored fabric bench which runs along all the walls around the room. On the right is a tall Arabic man accompanied by two others, all in white robes. This traditional robe is called a thobe. It is usually tailored like a shirt, but it is ankle-length and loose. One of the gentlemen must be his son. When he sees her, he calls her and her hubby into their room with a hand gesture. She is a little embarrassed to be wearing only capri pants and a tunica with short sleeves. Choosing to wear this in an international hotel is appropriate, because the main guests are tourists with only a few Arabians around them. The wife, who sits separately from the men on the left side of the room, gives her a smile and indicates that she may sit next to her while her husband is invited to join the men's corner.

She is relieved when she realizes that it's okay for this family, that because of her curiosity, she has been invited into this room, and they are not offended by her casual dressing.

They introduce themselves. The Arabic woman wears a headscarf that covers her head and shoulders, called a hijab.

The abaya is like a long black dress, but it is a robe that covers her body, and is usually made of black synthetic fiber, sometimes decorated with colored embroidery or sequins with a headscarf.

Even though they can't communicate in English that well, the connection is already there.

She gets invited to the men's corner where her hubby is talking with the Arabic men. They exchange business cards. Her hubby looks a little lost, because the communication skills between the senior Arabic man and him are quite poor. Not really understanding what is going on nor what they have been invited to the next day leaves them a bit apprehensive. They only know that they are expected in another emirate for lunch. The family leaves the hotel, and with them, the adventure has started.

QUESTIONS

- How open are you to wealth?
- What is luxury to you?
- Do you include all kinds of wealth in your life?
- What are they for you?
- Do you risk excluding people, family and friends, if you have more wealth or success in your life?
- What is your biggest fear about wealth?
- What is your biggest fear about success?
- What is your approach towards money?
- Where could you open up more to receive more abundance in your life?

There is family which you have been born into, there is extended family, and then there's a family collection of other people from the same culture and perhaps even from another culture with whom you have a connection. These effortless bonds are matching and occur naturally. It's about being open and ready to receive the diverse expression of life in the form of the individuality of humans. I feel so blessed to have experienced this kind of family. How about you?

ARABIC WORLD PART 2 - THE INVITATION

What do they bring with them as a gift? Where to get something out here in the desert where there are no shops? Arabs love good-quality chocolates wrapped in fancy silver or gold paper. They will get some on the way to their new friends. She is still asking herself whether this was a real invitation or whether it's just common courtesy in this culture. Perhaps they offered but did not expect them to accept or show up. Perhaps it's not even polite to accept it. They get informed by another Arabic man, an employee, that if someone from the Arab world offers you something, he means it.

She looks through all the clothes she has brought with her on her vacation. She never expected to have such an opportunity. She has a solution: a sleeveless black and white patterned dress, a bolero jacket to put over it, to cover her arms, and some black leggings to cover her legs.

In the morning they catch a taxi to their new friends who stay in the neighboring emirate, about an hour's drive from their hotel. The taxi driver gets lost and doesn't speak or understand English. They connect their friend with the taxi driver so that they can sort out how to get there. Unfortunately, this means that they can't stop and buy some delicious chocolates. For her it is very difficult to be invited somewhere and not bring a gift, but she can't change it; she must just surrender to it. She knows she will be able to give this wonderful couple the appreciation they deserve in another loving way.

They arrive at a parking lot, and he is waiting for them already. While welcoming her and her hubby very kindly, they enter his white Lexus, where, luckily, the air conditioning is running and cooling the car down. The seats are covered with plastic, which is quite irritating to her. Perhaps it's for practical reasons. This area is sandy and dusty after all. She doesn't know what to expect. Do they go straight to the restaurant, or does he have something else in mind? He drives them through the city; they love this private sightseeing city tour. It's rare to have a tour of this city without being exposed to the relentless heat. He stops at a small Arabic shopping mall. They get out of the car and walk as quickly as possible to the entrance to escape the humidity.

As they step into the mall, she realizes that they are the only foreigners there. All the salesmen are staring at her and her hubby. She feels more comfortable after asking her Arabic friend how appropriate it is for a foreign woman to walk with an Arabic man. His appearance as a tall and proud man is very impressive. He heads straight into the woman's clothing section. She is stressed out when he orders the shop owner to show her some colored thobes. Thobes are loose dresses which are worn over normal clothes with a scarf to match. She decides on a white dress which has colorful flowers on it and a pink scarf with the same flowers as the ones on the dress. He gifts this to her and hands it over to her in a shopping bag. She asks: *How can I accept this present from you?* He answers, *Because you now have a brother. I'm your brother from Kuwait and you are my sister.* She can't help herself; tears are running down her cheeks; she is so touched by his words. This unexpected openness towards her and her hubby is incredibly moving. It's an expression of unconditional love and acknowledgement, beyond any nationality.

Now it's the men's turn. Their brother from Kuwait buys a plain beige-colored thobe for her husband, not expecting him to wear it right now. He asks for a ghutra for himself, a headscarf, this time in checkered red and white.

It's so exciting not knowing where they will drive to after they finish the shopping trip. After a short drive by car, they find themselves in the business district of this modern city. They enter the tall business building and then the elevator, still not knowing where they will end up. The first few floors are all occupied by a bank. The elevator stops at the 14th floor. There is only his apartment on this floor. His wife opens the door wearing a black hijab and the scarf to cover her hair. She wears exquisite jewelry, and her fingertips are all orange; she used henna to tint them so that they are even more beautiful for the guests.

Now it's clear that they don't plan to go out to a restaurant. Instead, they'll stay at home and eat lunch at their apartment. It is very special for her to be invited to their private home. Their personal Indian cook from Kuwait follows them wherever they go. It's a win-win situation. The cook creates a delicious lunch, with a lot of different dishes. It all smells so delectable. There are only three plates on the table. She, her hubby and her brother from Kuwait are served. Her sister from Kuwait eats later, once her husband has eaten. This is very unusual to her; why shouldn't her sister eat at the same time as them? She realizes how their cultures differ.

Afterwards, they enjoy an Arabic coffee, served in a small cup that is adorned with a decorative pattern. Dates are offered to balance the bitter flavor. They use this opportunity to have a look outside the huge windows at the epic view of the modern buildings and the bay. She mentions to her brother that it's a privilege to have such a view and how lucky they are to have this apartment. She is embarrassed, and her cheeks start to blush, when she hears that her brother from Kuwait owns the whole building. What a dimension compared to her own life.

Together they enjoy the gathering, knowing that they have different religions and backgrounds. Because of the language barrier, it's not that easy to converse; but there is a deep connection beyond words.

QUESTIONS

- Is it easy for you to let someone new get close to you?
- What qualities should you display to feel more comfortable and safer to a foreigner?
- Where and when have you experienced acknowledgement, beyond any nationality?
- If you are invited somewhere, what would you bring as a gift?
- What could be an appealing alternative to a traditional gift?
- What is a unique skill that you bring with you to every gathering where no preparation is needed from your side? It could even be more than one.
- Where and when in your life have you experienced powerful and meaningful connections beyond words?

The home of person, yours and mine, is an expression and demonstration of our lifestyle, our standards, and what's important to us. It's a place for our wellbeing, both physical and emotional. To be invited into a friend's and even into a stranger's home is a factor of trust. I don't judge what is important to them and I will embrace the Universe which they allow me into in such a welcoming way. How open are you to different lifestyles and homes?

ARABIC WORLD PART 3 – QUALITY TIME

Her sister shows her the different rooms in their apartment. She explains that here in this emirate, they have much more modern classic furnishing than back at home in Kuwait. There they have a house with three different floors, and every storey has a unique color concept. While they walk through the rooms, her scarf is moved a little out of place and her wonderful black hair is exposed. They have a giggle. It's like a sisterhood, knowing they are safe and supported. She takes the opportunity to ask if she may touch her sister's hair. As a compensation, her sister may touch and feel her fine and short hair, too. They have a feast together. It's short and intimate. To have some time on their own, to talk about life, having children or not and agreeing that life is in Allah's hands is unforgettable. Even though she was brought up in a Christian culture, she decides to accept different names for God. It's so liberating to have diverse perspective and respect.

When they get back to the living room, she asks where the toilet is. Her brother replies: *Over there, but you have to know we don't have any water.* He was joking, but she nearly believed him. They had a good laugh together. Laughing is such a good way to bond.

When she comes out of the bathroom, she sees her brother kneeling on a small carpet, praying. Her first reaction is to just go back into the bathroom, hoping not to disturb him. He immediately gives her a sign that she may enter the living room; he has finished his prayer, and everything is more than fine.

The four of them get together to have an ice-cream wrapped in shiny paper. For her it's fascinating to see this fusion of modern and traditional lifestyle.

Her sister gets ready. She packs a small suitcase and sprays everyone with a freshening body splash that contains an alluring oriental scent.

She and her husband are informed that they will all be heading back to the desert resort and that they will take her and her hubby safely back to the hotel.

It's a lovely idea because they won't have to catch a taxi, and more importantly, will have more time to spend together. The brother, dressed in white with a headscarf, is driving; next to him sits her hubby wearing a white shirt and white pants, and on the back seat sits her sister, all in black. She herself is also dressed in the black bolero and the black and white dress. They feel like passengers on a joyride. On one hand, it's so unfamiliar, and on the other hand, it's so natural.

Suddenly her brother starts to sing a song only naming his wife's name, afterwards he starts singing her name, too. He repeats it several times, especially when he notices through the back mirror how touched she is. To hear her name sung out loud in such a loving, melodic way, opens her heart up even more. What high regards.

While the two men chat, the women chat, too. She asks her sister if she is able to drive a car and if she is allowed to. It is clear that her sister from Kuwait only travels first class. It's a different story for her who travels mostly economy! The fascinating part is that no matter how they differ in social and cultural status, they get on extremely well.

After driving on the highway, watching free camels walking along the side of the road, they arrive at the hotel. Two days ago, she wouldn't have been able to even dream of having such an adventure. She is so happy she accepted the invitation offered to her by her new sister and brother from Kuwait. The memories are especially momentous for her because she never had any siblings.

The resort has a special section for Arabic guests only. Those bungalows are built in a way that no one can look into the pool area or the terrace.

They will meet again in the morning for breakfast.

What an unbelievable day, what a gift and an unexpected adventure.

In the morning, they are looking forward to meeting their new friends again. Her sister is wearing the niqab. The niqab covers the face while leaving only the eyes uncovered. They get a table for four in a separate part of the restaurant. She is still astonished about the kind and caring way she and her hubby have been treated. What a setting: she now sits between the different worlds, the Arabic culture, the American culture, and every other culture in the restaurant.

While she and her sister get something from the buffet, she realizes how her sister gives the orders to the staff in a reserved way, a sort of *don't-look-at-me* kind of way. From her upbringing, she learned it's not polite to look away, instead she looks directly into the eyes of all the staff members. But she senses, from her sister, some freedom from her veil. Not being stared at as if she is she a sexual object is empowering. Her sister only opens the veil to eat or drink. For her, it's a challenge not to project something onto how her sister feels while she freely enjoys breakfast, however she wants to.

It's a once in a lifetime experience to be that close to someone who lives such a different life. He starts to sing her name again in the same manner he had before. It comes from both him and her sister's heart, even though he is the only one that actually sings. The energy of connection is there, it goes right into her heart, and her hubby can feel it too. It's time to say goodbye. Her brother and her sister are also touched by their meeting. All of them know it was such a precious and wonderful coincidence that brought them together in such a phenomenal way. Bliss and gratitude.

QUESTIONS

- What are some of your preconceptions about different cultures?
- Where would you like to be more open-minded, or even curious to learn more about a certain society?
- Do you question the pros and the cons about your own culture in which you grew up?
- What are they?
- Do you remember a situation with strangers in which your heart was touched by their kindness?
- To which foreign culture do you feel yourself drawn to, and why?
- Would you integrate some of their qualities into your own life?

Do you remember times where you or relatives of yours attended festive occasions where the classic ballroom dance was required? Or perhaps you were once a guest at a belly dancing performance or doing some belly dancing yourself? There are certain preferences, either you love to dance on your own or as a couple, or both. Perhaps you like to dress up for a dance event or maybe you are more of a spontaneous person and just love to dance wherever you are, whatever you're wearing, whenever you feel the need to. Wherever you are on this dancing scale, take a step into the world of expression through dancing.

LET'S DANCE

She loves music and she loves watching people dance. She was never that keen on dancing herself, especially since she has never felt able to freely move her body. She wasn't comfortable enough to let go and trust her dancing partners to guide her. Not that they wouldn't know how to lead; it was more about herself, her insecurity, feeling exposed and not knowing nor remembering the proper steps which are required for the different dances. When she and her hubby got married, they attended a dancing class. For her it was more than a confession of love from him to her. Her hubby joined her for a beginner's class even though he spent his tweens attending several amateur competitions. Having such a wide gap between absolute beginner and amateur was a lot for her. Being similar in height doesn't do the job, it only supports her view on what and how an attractive dance couple should look. They are opposites, not only on the dance floor, but in daily life, too. She is so lively and spontaneous, he, on the other hand, is calm and more introverted. She has to work on her expectations and let go of what society calls the right fit. Who has the right or is qualified to tell someone what the right match is, or give approval for a loving and enriching relationship? Every couple must find their unique way of living, find their own truth to live by their own standards. In the end they had the perfect wedding dance. She invited him for a salsa dance on an open space out in nature where she lost a small piece of her heel. Getting married or being committed to your spouse is a risk, but life itself is a risk, and even more so, an unpredictable gift. To dance through life together, for a short time or a lifetime, is always an adventure. There's no certainty that their personal developments will grow simultaneously or whether the joint path will suddenly divide into two. Whatever the case may be, it's always worth trying. She knows her partner is a great partner, a lover and a companion, the mirror and reflection in which she sees herself and once in a while, is shaken up and triggered, and vice versa. Even though ballroom dancing isn't really working for them as a couple, she and her hubby know they will certainty invite new adventures into their lives by dancing through life together.

She tries belly dancing. Not having to worry about a partner and only focusing on herself and the other women in the group might be easier. She loves the oriental music, the singing, the different instruments, the drums, and the rhythms. Diving deeply into the sensual world of expression of the female body, appreciating being a woman, is not about performing. It's about working with and experiencing her body in a different way. It's the whole package: the sensuality, being in the flow, creating soft and accentuated movements, being playful on one hand, but majestic on the other. Everything is mesmerizing: the colorful dancing clothes, the full-length skirts, the sensual flow of the fabric, the different styles, all the veils with sequin trims in every color imaginable. It's a world of infinite variety, and a paradise for goddesses. It's not easy to choose a hip scarf and belt with gold or silver coins on it; there are a lot of variations. These give weight to the hips and assist beginners to feel their hip movements better and helps to hear their own rhythm when preforming a movement like the shimmy. It's so much fun to learn to move with intention. The beginning was more a wiggle than it was a shimmy, but everything must be learned and practiced. Many of the moves in belly dancing involve isolations, which improves flexibility of the torso. Belly dancing moves include horizontal- and vertical-flowing figure-of-eights or infinity loops with the hips. Staccato movements, most commonly of the hips, are used to punctuate the music or accent a beat. You can't forget the shimmies, shivers, and vibrations. The arms are used to frame and accentuate movements of the hips, for dramatic effect, to create beautiful lines and shapes with the body. No wonder she can feel her muscles, they have to work. She feels so privileged to be a woman who is charmed by the shiny bracelets and cuffs, the anklets, the drop-chain chandelier rhinestone earrings. It's special to her to wear a navel belly jewel. She never dreamt she'd celebrate her navel, she actually always tried to hide her belly. She knows there is a celebrated background behind oriental dance and the sisterhood from ancient times. She is proud to be a woman, learning to accept and appreciate her body even more. To be in touch with the kind of dancing that matches her personality well is most important.

QUESTIONS

- What are some important qualities for an enriching love relationship?
- Are you totally clear about how you like to live, and with whom you would like to share your life with?
- What are your standards as a single person?
- Do you love to have some time on your own and even dance, move on your own?
- Do you love to get in touch with your sensuality while dancing on your own?
- Would you like to explore a more expanded world of sensuality, using scents, candles, fashion?
- Do you have a playlist of music which inspires you to dance? Why don't you add some different music styles to it?

Let's move it! Yes, even while you read this story, dance around in your mind; be barefoot so that you can feel the floor beneath you! Sense how your body enjoys moving to the different styles and rhythms of music. Sometimes, only reading about an activity inspires me to take action. How about you? There is no right or wrong way to do it, just the enjoyment to move and include your body in this expression of life.

5RHYTHMS DANCE

After connecting with belly dancing, she feels more confident. Confident enough to try all the different kinds of dancing. Her friend persuades her to join her for a 5Rhythms class. She is given the option to sit on the side and start dancing whenever she feels like she wants to join in.

She enters the large room with a wooden dance floor. There are dancers, both women and men, of all different ages, dressed up any way they like, sitting or lying on the floor, waiting for the class to resume. Most of them are barefoot. One of the rules here is, *No chit-chat during dancing.* The 5Rhythms are done in the following sequence: Flowing, Staccato, Chaos, Lyric and Stillness. One row is called a wave, two waves are danced during one event.

Gabrielle Roth, the founder of the 5Rhythms, says: It's about putting the body in motion in order to still the mind.

This kind of dance-practice confronts her as a dancer, with her self-imposed limitations, and invites her to explore new depths of creativity and connection. It creates a safe space to let fear, anger, sadness, joy and compassion be expressed as well.

She misses not being told what to do. She isn't told what steps or what order to do them in. She is fascinated by the fact that she often used to think how great it would be to not have to follow patterns or moves, and now that very option presents itself here at 5Rhythms. Its peculiar because she has a longing to be free, and out of nowhere, life comes along with this offer of freedom. As if she needed any more clarity. She looks around and sees how freely the dancers are expressing themselves; she feels lost in this space of endless possibilities. It's so freeing to get in touch with her body, and feel her strength, power, and agility, to contract and to expand. There are no right or wrong movements. No judgement. The only expectation is that she gets a little more in touch with herself. Another challenge she is confronted with is finding out whether she prefers dancing with a partner or on her own in this moment. She has to let go of all her perceptions, beliefs and worries about how she must act or perform while dancing with someone else. She must accept that there isn't a predictable outcome and that she must once again surrender and go with the flow. If she feels the need to stop before the song ends, she may do so, without explanation or guilt. It's a big learning curve, learning not to take everything so personally, or to try and hold onto a great connection and not let it go. It's also common for one to be concerned about their appearance and attractiveness while dancing, although with this dance, it's a totally different story. It is more alluring and more about getting in contact with one's own inner voice and soul. The appeal is in being authentic, not caring about how she looks when the music "of chaos" animates her to dance wildly and intensely. She has to admit that it's also not that easy to sweat in front of others, but if she wants to experience herself, and how it feels to be real and raw, this is the way. It's incredibly liberating for her to give herself the permission, to let go of shame, and to live out different aspects of life while loving it. It's wonderful to get a glimpse of it, and to experience herself while immersing herself in all the chaotic emotions. All 5rhythms, Flowing, Staccato, Chaos, Lyrical, Stillness, are welcomed, felt, and expressed through the dance, and even more so, the invitation to do so in her daily life as well.

QUESTIONS

- In what ways do you express fear, anger, sadness, joy, and compassion?
- Do you express them by dancing, singing, painting, or in another way?
- Are you in alignment with your personality and the ways you move?
- How do you allow your inner tigress or tiger to come out, by not holding back but instead getting into action?
- Do you use your body to support your mental health? Where could you include your body even more?

To do a sport in a group can be very entertaining and quite energizing. It is also a training session, not only physically but emotionally too. Although there is no need, the temptation to compare and compete will arise. To stay connected with yourself and to just be proud enough that you are competing is what really counts. To be able to rejoice with others in the group is significant too.

OUT INTO THE SNOW – BACKCOUNTRY SKIING

She loves being out in the snow. She and her hubby sign up for a tour with a special alpine club. It's a friendly winter morning; the sun is up but it's still cold. They meet at the parking lot close to a specific mountain. Once more she and her hubby check to make sure that they have everything they need for their backcountry skiing tour. For a whole day out in the snow, different layers of functional clothes will be needed. As well some victuals and warm tea.

The participants are divided into two groups: one for the more advanced and one for the beginners.

They start preparing. The skins which are put underneath the skis are made either from synthetic nylon, mohair (hair from Angora goats) or a blend of the two. The role of these skins are traction and glide.

Special touring bindings including some climbing aids are needed to go up the steep hills. Activating the climbing aids feels as though she is in high heels. This thought is especially amusing if she considers that there are more men in the group than women. Women haven't really been welcomed for too long, it was more of a gentlemen-only club before, but to everyone's relief, this has changed. There are also some female guides now.

The backcountry skiing boots are already more flexible than the racing ski boots are. She must still make an adjustment and uses a softer tongue in her shoe to prevent her from having pain in her shins. It's all about adaptation and personal adjustment.

One of her friends is their guide, and he explains: *It's important not to get pressured by the more advanced participants. They might have the technical skills but they're missing the social competence and interaction. Don't look to the front of the groups as a newbie, it always seems that those leading are hours ahead and that it will take you forever to reach your goal. But that's not actually the case. You will get to the peak no more than a few minutes after they do. As long as you walk at your own pace, you will not get worn out. You will also enjoy a pause to recover at the summit. You will see the amazing view down to the valleys, the other wonderful peaks around you, and the companionship with the others too.*

No one likes to be last, but everyone is more than relieved that there are those in the group who are less experienced, slower, and not as strong as they are. Competition is everywhere. In the middle of the tour, he suggests that she takes over his place as the head of their group, following the tracks which the group in front of them have created. She enjoys herself while going along tracing the steps to the finish line.

She tries to use some affirmations: *I have enough oxygen in my cells and muscles, I regenerate while I'm walking, I have double the amount of the energy I need for this powerful physical engagement. My body feels great and loves to workout in this way.* She adapts it as she goes: *I have more than enough energy left.... It's working.* When they approach the top, a decision is made by the guides to take an alternative route. Although they are quite close to their goal, they may have to go down as the risk of an avalanche is too high.

In a situation like this, to be that close to the goal yet so far, needs a strong mind. The pride and the "FOMO", fear of missing out, must be set aside to instead take responsibility and have the courage to change it, regardless of everyone's opinion. Safety first. Every situation has the potential to be a learning experience.

Now they have to cross through a steep hillside, using skin track kick-turns, a technique which is an awkward-looking maneuver that's even more awkward to perform. It helps to change direction on a steep mountainside. She knows she must exercise caution so as not to slip down the hill and potentially set off an avalanche. She gets encouraged and supported by the more advanced group members. What a relief, after the struggle of having to perform several of those maneuvers.

They continue where the conditions are better and safer. They enjoy the time in the snow, enjoying the sunshine and the fresh air.

Nothing is more satisfying or adrenaline-enhancing than sliding downhill with skis on a virgin snowy mountain.

Not really considering each other, most of the group attempt to seize the opportunity first.

The best skier enjoys being at the end of the group. He takes care of the safety of everyone, gives support when needed and celebrates the success of the beginners. She appreciates his strength and not needing to show off or put others down, instead helping them to take the next step up to the next level. Victory for both small and huge achievements.

QUESTIONS

- Do you use affirmations? What are yours?
- Do you use afformations by asking positive questions? What are they?
- Do you enjoy adapting and adjusting for personal growth? Do you include them in all areas of your life?
- Are you driven by "FOMO", the fear of missing out?
- What's your solution to it?
- What are some powerful and uplifting tools which work for you, to overcome feelings of being broken, and not good enough?
- Do you celebrate the small victories in your life as well the huge achievements? Just do it and enjoy it!

Have you ever attended a personal development event not really knowing what to expect? Getting out of your comfort zone and being honest about your flawed beliefs, self-doubts, and fears? To gain a clear understanding of what your limitations and boundaries are? If not, why don't you join her?

PERSONAL DEVELOPMENT EXERCISES

Glass Walk Challenge

She attends a one-day workshop in personal development and is looking forward to the nuggets of enlightenment she will receive. They never mentioned anything about a glass walking challenge. She does think that it was probably better to find out on the day of the event rather than before. Who knows if she would have even attended the workshop if she had had time to overthink it? She is content because she knows she has the free will to do it or not. It's a comfortable atmosphere. The workshop leader has the skills to mentally prepare the participants for the glass walk challenge. They are divided in several small groups. She can sense the energy level building up in her body and the rest of the room too. She learns that in order to accomplish this, it will be necessary to change her thought processes about the negative aspects of glass we have come to accept as truth, as well as any associated thoughts related to the glass itself. Think of the glass as cotton wool, or any other soft material. It's about engaging the mind-body connection. Set on the stage are four meters of smashed sterilized glass wine bottles. It looks similar to a path. The first people walk over it barefoot. Now its her turn. She takes off her socks, looks at her bare feet, centers herself, and focusses on a visual goal. She controls her breathing and walks without hesitation; she moves confidently over the glass carpet. She comes away unscathed, having overcome her fears. Satisfaction, but on a more rewarding level. It's an unforgettable experience on her journey to a greater understanding of how to break down subconscious and deep-routed fears. It was an unbelievable achievement expanding her prejudiced perceptions of what she can and cannot accomplish.

Trust exercise

She likes to educate and better herself by attending personal development workshops. This one is very hands-on. The group is small, and the whole setting is for one exercise: the well-structured trust-fall exercise. It is commonly used in seminars, team building and body-mind processes. The exercise will take place on a wooden construction platform, around two meters high. The leader stands up on the wooden platform to welcome the participant and prepare them mentally. They will deliberately fall backwards into the interlocked arms of the whole group. She isn't particularly keen to do the exercise. She allows everyone to go before her to see that everyone, no matter their size, is safely caught. She senses how her anxiety, abandonment, and loss of control come up while procrastinating the actual performance. She asks herself why she waits to go last. In a way, it makes her feel even more nervous watching everyone go before she does. She can feel their tautness, and this creates a struggle in her attempts to stay centered. It's her turn. She climbs up with shaky legs, her back facing the fall area. She faces the instructor who is trying to connect with her. She feels cared for, knowing she will not be forced and will be allowed to go whenever she is ready. He will give her a gentle nudge while she stands, arms crossed in front of her chest, body erect and body tense. Her self-doubts are gone; instead, her mind is on a mission. It is the time to receive. What a positive impact this has on her. She takes a step forward by taking a step back and lets go of her concerns about others. It crosses her mind, *What if I am too much for others?* Is her mentality: *Are you ready for me? Here I come, with my whole presence and all my power.*

QUESTIONS

- How important is it for you to have autonomy?
- Do you remember powerful situations where you didn't hesitate at all and stood up for yourself or others, with a lot of confidence?
- Do you have a clear mission on your mind of how you would like to experience yourself now and in the future?
- Where would you like to improve, get more self-esteem, self-assurance and poise?
- How does your life in the following areas look: health and fitness, relationships, business, and personal growth?
- What will it look like if you don't hold yourself back anymore?
- How is your presence, appearance, and power?
- What is the risk of doing so and what will you gain and contribute to others?

How about creating a challenge for yourself with clear rules and then sticking to them? You don't have to report to anyone, its only you that you are committing to, and it's an act of self-determination which is no one's concern except yours. It's your goal to get to know yourself a little better. One more step towards your true self and empowering yourself.

ON THE ALPS

She knows she doesn't feel comfortable staying at a hotel on her own. Especially if its more on the wild side, up in the mountains. She occasionally still gets anxiety.

Challenge accepted! The challenge which she creates for herself is as follows: Some Don'ts: 1. No phone except for in an emergency, so there are none of the usual distractions like getting in contact with the outer world, watching videos, texting, or listening to music. 2. No Laptop 3. No books. Some okay's are: 4. Notebooks and a pen. 5. She has to eat on her own 6. She must hike on her own, barefoot when possible 7. No unnecessary conversations.

It's too easy to get into a conversation with other people. The task is simple: To be alone and to feel comfortable with herself as a companion. She feels like it's the right decision. She wants to challenge herself and stick to the rules she created for the next two days. It already feels like a week. Others would love to have some "me" time and dream of having the opportunity to be on their own, and she doesn't feel guilty about it. She will be confronting her fears of being on her own, not knowing whether she can cope with the recurring anxiety. She gives herself leeway to not be pushed into any situation unless she is comfortable that the experience will help her in her personal development. She is aware that she will have nearly no distractions, only time to sit with her mind, chat with nature, and be in the present.

She decides to book a hotel room up in the mountain on an alp. After a 1.5 hour drive, she arrives at the base of the village. She heads up a small bumpy road which leads to the alp and has to be careful that the underbody of the car doesn't get caught or damaged from the rocks and the unevenness of the path. When she reaches the flat surface of the alp, she finally sees green wonderland. It's fall, and already there's some snow on the fields. She parks her car close to the mountain hotel and knowing that she can leave whenever she pleases gives her peace. The hotel has a few rooms, and they are all cozy with a lot of wood. She makes herself comfortable in her room. The windows are positioned towards a huge field where a small creek flows by. It's so quiet and peaceful. She goes outside for a walk before it gets dark, and the dinner is served. She looks at those amazing different moors. It's a nature park with a lot of variants of moors. The color of the glorious nature uplifts her mood; the worries are slowly melting away. It's time for dinner and she gets a table on her own. Couples and small groups are eating and enjoying each other's company. She takes something along with her to write with. She wants to make sure that should she get uncomfortable or bored with herself, that she is able to entertain herself by writing or sketching notes. This is like her personal-aid kit. She enjoys a delicious meal and a glass of red wine.

Before she goes to bed, she looks outside the window. It's black; nothing to see but a canvas of shining stars that are sparkling in the distance.

After she's completed her evening rituals, she goes to bed and sleeps wonderfully.

When she gets up in the morning, she knows she is ready to do the hike. While walking on the hike path along the meadows, she is met with beautifully arranged moorland lakes, crystal-clear streams, and the fresh air and charm of the alps. She feels wonderful, adventurous, and free on her own. She crosses a creek and takes off her shoes. It's time for her to walk barefooted and feel the earth, the grass, even some snow and stones under her feet. It's meditation, "her way" of meditation. She is so proud for giving herself the space to experience something much bigger than her fear and allowing herself to experience real connection with her own power and source in such a simple and effortless way.

QUESTIONS

- Where and when do you shame yourself for being a certain way, with certain needs and insecurities?
- Where do you like to just fit in?
- Where have you not made peace with who you are?
- Where would you cheer someone else up, but not give yourself the same empathy?
- Do you have a special kit, a personalized aid kit, that gives you the support you need whether on vacation, on a special adventure, or in the process of stepping out of your comfort zone?
- Is it a material kit or a mental kit, or both? What does it contain?
- What are your morning rituals?
- What are your evening rituals?
- What about creating a small challenge for yourself, with clear rules that you come up with? Something which nourishes your soul and will make you rejoice afterwards.

Have you tried spending some quality time with a close friend of yours in an unconventional way? Do you always meet at the same place, or do you like to have a variety of settings? I love those rejoicing moments, knowing we have so much to share. As if time stands still. It's not about the food, even though it can be very nice to share some delicious food together. It's more about real connection and vulnerability, supporting each other, motivating each other, and abundant empathy. And don't forget the giving and receiving of input to make life even more colorful and easier to take.

PICNIC PART 1

What about having a picnic? It's a relaxing and chilled social event. She loves being inspired by her close American friend who is extremely spontaneous and fun to be with. Getting together is more about the quality time spent being in each other's company than it is the buffet.

A small gathering created with such simplicity. It is such a blast bonding with her friend, and nourishing to their friendship too. The two women love to chat and share insights about their challenges and what they are up to and encourage each other with feedback. Why not share, care and eat at the same time!

When they get together, they always have an adventure. They love to go out into nature and sit at the lake to reboot, watching the enticing blue water. They also enjoy going into the woods to cool down when the sun is too intense. They find a nice place like a tree trunk to sit on or a grill place where there are wooden picnic benches and tables. It's a good place to be because they are both very lively and love to be able to shout out if something excites them, or sing out loud if they feel like it, not hold their laughter back. It is a real freedom to be able express themselves and receive acceptance from each other just by being themselves. A real sisterhood, with all its divine secrets.

The two women are prepared for an excursion. They get something to eat like a salad with different ingredients and separate plates to share it. If they buy sandwiches, they will divide them in half and use a napkin as a plate. It's also fine if they do not get something to share and each choose something suitable for themselves. They will sip on a refreshing sparkling water and enjoy what nature has provided. Why not spoil themselves with an easy dessert too? Some refreshing watermelon, some delicious chocolate wrapped in nice shiny paper, or some sensual strawberries are usually the final topping on this cake. The ambiance of celebration is in the air. A celebration of life.

It's so uncomplicated and hassle-free. Her friend doesn't even care if her white blouse gets dirty or gets some stains on it. It often happens this way. Perhaps an olive happily makes its way down her blouse, or some tomato sauce will create a red art piece on her shirt. Either way, it's not unexpected. Her friend teaches her not to care about what could happen and live trying to prevent it. If it happens, then she will sort it out, but she won't worry about it beforehand. There is always a solution to it. Her friend often reminds her to stay in the present.

Her friend once messed up her white blouse, went home to wash and hang it outside on the improvised balcony to dry. It was quite windy, and when she came back outside, the blouse was hanging on the next tree! That's life, that's living, accept it and find joy.

QUESTION

- What is important in your friendships?
- How do you cultivate those precious friendships?
- What are ways you like to experience friendship?
- What is sisterhood or brotherhood to you?
- Are you aware of the great gift you are as a friend?
- What lessons have been taught to you by a friend?
- Who do you share insights and treasures with?
- How do you like to celebrate life and friendship?

When last did you go on a picnic? Was it just organizing a playful gathering out in the woods, on the beach, in a meadow full of flowers, in a city park, on a boat, at a river, up in the mountains? Food is always a nice and easy way to connect with other people. A picnic is a very personalized expression of creativity, from a very opulent buffet to a more relaxed one. There is no right or wrong. It's about a relaxed gathering with friends, inviting humor, having a chat, and when the time is right, some philosophical moments may even emerge. Being open to other lifestyles is one way to win in life. A romantic tête à tête with your spouse is also always a highlight, leaving daily life behind and focusing on each other as a couple. Just have a picnic!

PICNIC PART 2

Food, habits, and rituals are important in every culture. Picnics are one of these rituals and can be experienced in so many ways.

She invites a close friend of hers to celebrate her birthday with a picnic on the pier at the lake. The month of May is still not high season, so they will have the whole pier to themselves. Sitting with blankets, they make themselves comfortable on the small wooden paradise. She hears small waves passing underneath the pier, while placing the lovely, prepared dishes in bowls with napkins on the picnic blanket. They don't need background music it's already included with the splashing of the water and the gaggle of the ducks. Because her friend loves vegetarian food, she got a great selection from a vegan restaurant. It looks very appetizing. For her it's important that she gifts people with things that are meaningful to them. It's about pleasing them and not her.

Another way she loves to picnic is when she is invited to a friend's house to sit on their lovely, decorated terrace with them. It's designed like a lounge, and it's like being on vacation, surrounded with green plants, cushions, lamps and candles and those romantic water glasses and mezze. Her friend likes to cook, decorate, and host, and she likes to flood her friend with gratitude. So, it's a win-win situation! Enjoying this relaxed gathering while sipping on a glass of lemon water, Prosecco, or wine. It's so precious and lovely to be together and speak vulnerably with no judgement. Sharing the challenges which come up for all of them, as individuals and as couples in daily life. Holding space for one another in this world, safe space without judgement, is a step towards true freedom for us all.

A couple's picnic can be just as sacred.

When she and her hubby were in the desert resort they booked a romantic picnic out in the desert, where there were no other people, only the night, the moon, and thousands of stars. The staff organized a picnic, a real one-thousand-and-one-night picnic, with a huge Arabic carpet, lots of cushions and a low table in the center of it. They sat on the floor and used some cushions to support their sitting position. The staff fixed some way torches at all the corners of the carpets as well as lit some candles to give it a more romantic atmosphere. While they made themselves comfortable, still curious about what the chef had prepared for them, they were introduced to the Arabic menu. Everything was perfectly organized, one box for the dishes which had to be served warm and another for the beverages and dessert. The staff took off with their Jeep and left the couple on their own. They were given a radio device and informed when they would be picked up again. Adventure and silence were in the air. They looked around, there was only sand and dunes and the two of them. It was serene and slightly scary at the same time. But they found comfort being with each other, which was the goal.

A picnic up in the mountains is also just as satisfying, especially during an intense hike. She and her hubby love to be active in nature and to take picnics on their travels. They sit down on the grass or on a flat stone and enjoy the homemade sandwiches, nuts, dried fruits, a banana, or even some chocolate as a dessert while taking in the beauty of the astonishing majestic mountains. When they are brave enough, they take a footbath in a chilly mountain stream.

To picnic, to eat together, and to connect with each other can be experienced in so many different ways, in so many different countries and cultures.

QUESTIONS

- What do picnics and parties mean to you?
- What kind of picnics do you enjoy hosting?
- Do you prefer to be invited to a picnic or party as a guest, do you like to give a hand to the host, or do you like to host the event yourself?
- What is the win-win situation for you when having a gathering?
- Do you love creating a nice, decorated dinner table when you and your spouse are alone?
- What about having an evening out as a couple, like when you first met each other?
- Do you still organize surprises, candlelit dinners, and romantic evenings for you and your spouse? Do great ideas come to you right now? Write them down.
- How can you renew and spice up your relationship? Put down some ideas to grab if needed.

Flow sounds good, but first the barriers of tension must be broken through. I often do this by consciously lowering my limiting-belief barriers and simultaneously gaining more confidence and more courage to let go of what is holding me back from the long-awaited, much anticipated result.

FLOW TRAIL

Once in a while she tries a seriously adventurous challenge. Mountain biking is her next choice. The teacher is a young, friendly, and very sporty woman with blonde braids. Her hubby is joining her. With helmets and protective gear in place, the journey is underway. She asks for a special pedal that has two different sides. On one side your foot isn't fixed to the pedal, so it's easy to get on and off. On the other side is the real deal where your foot clicks in. Just as in life, there are always two sides of a coin. The latter gives the biker the more direct connection to the bike, with the security that if she jumps or rides over an obstacle, her feet won't slip off the pedal. The second option is more convenient for people like her who are more afraid that they could fall off the bike. Especially when they have to stop suddenly, and they're not quick enough to click out, or they forget that they are attached in the first place. Nothing will help them stop the slow-motion sideway fall to the floor. Safety first is her motto.

Balancing exercises followed by maneuvers. Breathing always helps, especially if she feels overwhelmed and tense while learning the new skills.

During the parkour, she gets fired up by the enthusiastic young teacher.

Trying and failing is how she has learnt most things her whole life. After a while she needs to rest and consciously realign her mindset with her goal.

Every cell of her being celebrates this first success. But another challenge is already waiting for her. After having learned the basics, she and her hubby, accompanied by the blonde instructor, attempt their first flow trail. It's sometimes good for her to not really know what she is saying "yes" to.

She is encouraged to give this a try because there are no tourists around, and the trail is free for beginners. None of the ambitious sports junkies will show up either.

That sounds very appealing to her.

Following close behind the instructor, she holds onto the brakes and braces the whole bike tightly with her legs. She tries to get up and off the seat, and even behind the seat when it gets very steep. The goal is to maintain her center of gravity. Using this technique helps her balance the bike better and avoid getting overthrown when using the brakes on the steep areas.

Because she is so nervous, she uses the brakes very frequently. Her fingers are nearly limp because she tells herself it's better to be safe than sorry. She uses so much pressure to squeeze the brakes, it is as if she is squeezing an unripe lemon by hand. To her surprise, the path is quite steep for a beginner. Sometimes she has to pause and regain her courage to continue on with this adventure. In one spot she has to use her bike to jump up onto a step which leads to a path which is made out of wooden panels. The panel course is surrounded with small green bushes. There are no real risks, even if she were to fall into the bushes. She grinds to a halt when she stops and sees this wooden trail. She gets off the bike and walks back up the hill to give it another try. Another brief safety check and off she goes. She gets to the same point where she struggled before and she hits the brakes again. Once more it's the same procedure. She talks encouragingly and kindly to herself. While the correct equipment is vital, more importantly, the right mindset is the key to success here. By not underestimating yourself, just one step out of your comfort zone can open a new world to you. She loves personal development, and now she is in the middle of it. She hears herself saying: *Your mindset has to change or the result will stay the same.*

She takes a deep breath and starts riding towards the fear, not like a biking pro, but more like someone who isn't giving up. She gives herself the chance to overcome an obstacle.

She must have enough speed to successfully get over the panel course and drive through it. This time it's a victory! What an experience to be in the flow on an actual flow trail. What success and what joy. An explosion of energy describes it best. She dedicates a full portion of appreciation towards herself and gratitude towards the instructor. The instructor says it has never taken her that long to ride this trail and that she has never had as much fun and connection as she had with her and her hubby. To share the joy and the success is so wonderful and so satisfying. Now that they are off their bikes, they can fully take in the magnificent scenery in which she and her hubby were biking. They had been focused on the trail, heads down, but now they have all the time to look up, look around, be grateful for the whole adventure and enjoy the wonderful and beautiful lakes and mountains.

Peace and freedom. Once more it was worth it to step out of their comfort zones into the unknown to explore one more facet of life.

QUESTIONS

- What success of yours comes to your mind that would be so fun and satisfying for you to share?
- What is required for you to step out of your comfort zone?
- What do you do when you feel overwhelmed while learning a new skill or a new sport?
- Are you ready to change your mindset in certain areas of your life to pursue different and more satisfying results?
- What tangible goals would you like to set and accomplish?
- What adventure would you like to experience, even if it means that you must overcome your fear and doubts or leave your comfort zone?
- How must your mindset towards this goal shift in order to get there?

What is your relationship with fashion? Is it exciting for you to reinvent yourself by wearing something which you never considered a good match, or makes you feel a certain way? Do you like to express yourself by wearing different styles, or are you more of a person who likes to be practical and go with the familiar? There are as many styles as there are stars in the sky. It's wonderful to dress yourself in a way which suits your personality, your lifestyle, and most importantly, spark more joy into your daily life. Let's go shopping.

ST. MORITZ PART 1 - SHOPPING

She doesn't know what she should expect, only that she loves having "grown up girls" experiences, while stepping out of her comfort zone. One fact is clear: She has been invited to an event at a 5-Star hotel in St Moritz, but she doesn't have anything to wear to the lavish occasion.

She doesn't really feel at home in high-society circles. She knows how to carry herself, but this is definitely not her world. For her a person's family background and title are not important, nor what material possessions they have in this world, but rather, their hearts and how they treat other people. Visiting a boutique with a good friend of hers who is familiar with this kind of dress code feels like a safe way to explore this new territory. Glittering and shiny dresses hang everywhere when they enter the store. At the entrance, a high-collar gown demands her attention. The long dress is animal print. Roar! The touch of the fabric is too wonderful, soft, and sensual for words. Let's stretch it, babe. It takes all her courage to try it on - even if it's only to see herself as a different character. Wow, what cleavage! Surprised by her own guts, she steps out of the dressing room into the middle of the boutique.

There is excitement and flattery from her friend and the shop owner at first. But then a few seconds later, an answer to a question not even asked cuts right through her courage. The owner offers inappropriate criticism: *Despite the fact that it's your natural hair, not dyed and not grey, your hair is boring. Something has to change - you have to be spiced up. The shapewear women now have access to is great and helps to keep everything snug and tight.* She is shocked. Instead of feeling empowered, she feels like she is drowning. She still feels the loving touch of the material and the tigress that is embracing her body with this wonderful fabric trying to suppress her tears.

Her confidence, upright posture, and inner glow have vanished. Back in the dressing room, not having even closed the curtains properly, her eyes stare into the mirror, and she examines her reflection. Digesting the comments, she feels so weak and unlovable. She hears herself saying, *Why don't you get it, they are only trying to bring out the best in your appearance and your personality?* What if they are right with their comments, what if the way she looks isn't okay? Should she consider hair implants, now that menopause is affecting so many different parts of her body? Perhaps she should consider having her hair dyed (like she used to for several years, to have it in all shades of red) even though up until now it has been so freeing not being dependent on it anymore. Is she unattractive if she isn't taking advantage of the innovations of the modern world? A world in which being perfect, at least from the outside, has so much value? What's perfect, anyway? Her inner dialogue continues. *Aren't we women trying to free ourselves, claiming to regain our power, while restricting our uniqueness by trying to fit into a system of society and consumerism?* Another unstoppable thought inevitably appears: Should she perhaps, as recommended, wear a piece of lingerie which tightens her hips and belly? She remembers how she once gave this a try when she and her hubby stayed at a fancy hotel and went out for a fancy dinner in the restaurant hotel. During the aperitif, she got up, went back to her hotel room, and substituted her shapewear for some more appealing underwear. She went back downstairs and enjoyed every bite of the delicious food and the way her body felt, accepted and wonderful. Isn't the real freedom deciding to wear whatever is right for ourselves? Accepting our bodies, our shapes, the ways our bodies change through pregnancies, menopause, illnesses and aging? Not betraying ourselves or our authenticity, but rather celebrating how body and soul positivity and harmony with the ebbs and flows of life is the path to our inner peace? While she climbs out of the new, fun, and stylish tigeress dress, she asks herself: *Why don't women know that they won't lose anything for themselves, but will gain a whole universe, if they are supportive and nourishing to each other?* This tigress dress is a symbol of her true power and beauty. She wants to be able to wear this dress whenever she feels like it, whenever she needs to be reminded of the tigress within. This dress will tell the story of how she overcame her doubts and fought against the low self-esteem that threatened to steal her peace. This dress will tell the story of how she freed herself from not feeling good enough. She can snuggle in it or go out for a date with her hubby. She feels sexy and feminine and brave.

This was a painful, unpleasant experience, but a good life lesson. On that day she made up her mind that she would never allow anyone to make her feel this way again.

Now she is more aware than ever that it is up to her to be clear about her boundaries, and when necessary, find the courage to stand up and speak up for herself. What a relief to experience self-love in such a way. The tigress was always a part of her- the dress only reminded her of the power she already had within.

QUESTIONS

- How do you like to feel about yourself when you are in society?
- What best represents your personality?
- What kind of material do you like to feel on your skin?
- What are the colors you feel comfortable in?
- Is your style unique?
- What clothes make you feel powerful?
- What stories do you attach to certain clothes?
- Are you already accepting of your body, your shape, and the ways your body changes during different seasons of life?
- How do you celebrate your body and soul positivity?

Lifehack: Why not challenge yourself by being perfectly imperfect.

Are you an early bird? Do you like to be in nature as the day softly begins to reveal itself? The moments when it is quiet, and the rest of the world is still sleeping? Can you imagine how it would feel to experience this out on the lake, gliding across the water? It's spiritual.

ST. MORITZ PART 2 – SUP

The refreshing cool breeze of the morning and the fog which hangs over the lake of St. Moritz, up in the mountains in Switzerland, is welcoming.

It's time to give this small, charming lake a try. She arrives at the sailing club to rent a SUP – a Stand Up Paddleboard. One of the staff members assists her in getting the heavy board down from the special racks where all the other boards are lined up. She carries the board as quickly as possible straight to the landing dock where the rowing boats are launched. During this short sequence of lifting and getting the board to the shore, her arms feel as though they are growing longer and longer. Her grip is awkward, and her muscles aren't used to it. Everything has its pros and cons. Especially when getting out of one's comfort zone. She makes sure that her sporty tight clothes are in place, and that they are flexible enough to allow her to move around with ease and protect her if she loses her balance and falls into the cold mountain water. She adjusts her paddle to the correct height.

It's a carbon lightweight version that she bought for herself. She tried rental paddles before but holding them and trying to maneuver with them felt as though she was weightlifting with a weight bar. Why not choose the perfect size and material with a comfortable handle? Even the style and color are important for someone who is as esthetic as she is.

Off she goes. Starting on her knees, she keeps her eyes directed straight ahead to help her balance. This helps her to get up quickly and use the paddle to find the balance. Every stroke splashes water on her ankles and into her five-finger shoes. It's chilly. She holds her breath for a second and then goes on, knowing everything has its price and it's worth having cold feet to experience such a beautiful expression of nature. It's truly fulfilling. She passes a couple who are also on their SUPs. They tell her that she must flip the paddle to give her the opportunity to speed up. She tries to be open minded, even though she had a lesson with a pro and learned the different maneuvers and skills to paddle better than most beginners do. But she agrees to try and switches it up. Of course, the recommendation from this couple isn't working. Luckily for the couple, the wind is coming from behind and is supporting them, but she on the other hand has the wind coming head-on. She will enjoy the push of the wind from behind on her return.

Who is she trusting, herself or others? While she still has her mind on those thoughts, the sail regatta is preparing to launch and the boats are ready. She is comfortable because she knows she is not in their way. She is so grateful to be on this lake early in the morning, basking in the amazing scenery around her. The mountains still have snow on their peaks, with a few tourists walking by on the path beside the lake. She looks around and up to St.Moritz with its four imposing and legendary 5-Star hotels that touch the shore.

What a gift. The fresh air and the sound of the paddle pushing through the water is sensational. The board glides smoothly on the glassy surface of the water. Occasionally she passes some rowers doing their morning workout. It's all just pure freedom.

She turns around in the shallow water near shore and spots seagrass flowing and dancing around with the current. As she approaches the starting point, she hears the staff of the regatta shouting from a distance towards her: *Hey, you have your paddle the wrong way around!* Oh, not again. Someone is telling her what she should do and what is right and what is wrong. She is so tired of getting advice without asking for it. She hears herself asking: Who is the owner of this paddle? She is! And she even had a pro teach her the technique as well as the correct position of the paddle. So, who is in charge here? That's a question she often has on her mind. Who is she listening to? She makes her message loud and clear when she shouts back: "It's my paddle and I know how to use it!"

Just because someone thinks he or she is an expert in something, or worse, in everything, it doesn't mean that's really the case. Now he gets it. Because of the angle of the sunlight, the shovel curvature of the paddle seems different to the usual look of other paddles. He had the wrong perspective.

"You are right!" he shouts towards her, acting like the lake sheriff. It was worth it, not giving in or up on herself and her voice in that moment, instead boosting her self-esteem by being assertive and standing firm with her boundaries. What a success. She is so proud of herself. She stuck to her truth and didn't get caught up in feeling insecure around a person who tells others what's right and what everyone should do.

It's about owning her truth and using her voice. It's about self-respect.

QUESTIONS

- Do you give yourself the freedom to choose what is right for you and what is a right fit for you?
- In which areas have you already chosen to be true to yourself, and where do you want to adjust?
- What about in your living space with what belongs in it? Your clothes, your sport equipment, and of course your daily routines (and so much more)?
- How do you react when getting advice you haven't asked for?
- Where do you find yourself giving advice and making assumptions without being asked?
- Who do you trust more, yourself or others?
- Where do you need your messages to be stronger and clearer, to make sure that you are heard and understood?
- In what areas of your life do you want to be more precise and certain to assert stronger boundaries?

Lifehack: Be aware, everything has its pros and cons.

Are you open to getting your hands dirty? Are you ready to sweat, dig deep, and try a new kind of workout? Be taken back to a time and technique that has become popular again.

BUILDING A SAUNA

A close friend of hers tells her about his new project. He is building a natural sauna. She is interested in all sorts of creations, handcrafts, and native expressions. She knows she must get uncomfortable and put on her hat of open-mindedness to be able to take on whatever the Universe brings her. She prefers to not get dirty or live too rustically, but she is fascinated by the different ways people live and explore life and nature. For her it's always a gift when someone invites her into their Universe, knowing there's no need to fake something or pretend like she belongs to it. She would rather show curiosity so she can understand what is important for some and why they live their personal lives the way they do. What makes them choose this kind of lifestyle. Thanks to her ability to receive, she gets to experience so many different people and is privileged to be part of new experiences and leave whenever it's time for her to go back into her own world. She feels both privileged and tested in life. Her insecurities are sometimes exposed when taking risks, comparing herself with others or justifying her own way of living.

She gets ready to visit him at his home in nature. She decides to wear clothes which can get dirty or torn. The location is close to the woods and a natural waterfall. It's positioned in an idyllic spot; it fits well with the surroundings. It's the right place for a sauna. Her friend started the project weeks before, and she is here to help him to get a little further. She knows he loves the way the sauna evolves in front of his eyes. No rush and no stress. She sees a large cover lying on the grass. Her friend explains to her what the next step will be. First, he places the earthy material on the plastic covering sheet and adds some water to it. They remove the bigger stones out of the muddy mixture and walk around barefoot in the mud to mix it. Their toes dig into the slippery material to feel for stones that must be picked up and discarded. It feels like a form of meditation and a great opportunity to talk to each other in an uncomplicated way. She is already wearing a sunhat; its midsummer and it feels similar to hot yoga. After they have taken all the stones out, he spreads some sand and straw, all in the right proportion to create the correct consistency. For her it's like baking a cake: the dough must be kneaded. Similarly, this must happen to create the clay. All their muscle power is needed to lift the cover sheet with the heavy dampened clay and move it to the middle. They repeat the procedure until the clay is mixed well and ready to be used for the walls of the sauna. Moving it from its current position to where the sauna is going to be built is exhausting. What an adventure. She feels as though she has stepped back in time, thrown back into an earlier epoch, using raw materials from nature to build, to create. Nothing is prefabricated. He cuts logs into smaller pieces which will become the walls. With their bare hands they put a layer of clay on the dried wall, then the wood is put on and fitted in. Some big stones which he carefully chose from the riverbed are inserted, too. Every newly added material must be cemented with the clay. Some colorful bottoms from different kinds of glass bottles are added too. The sunlight will shine through the different colors of glass to create a kaleidoscope inside the sauna.

She couldn't care less about how much she sweats or how worn out she looks, or how much mud and clay she has all over her. To do such hands-on work is a transcending experience. It's unbelievably satisfying to be a part of an alchemistic task. It is so fulfilling to connect with nature and with this beautiful friend. It's a heart-warming feeling to create a sauna which will serve many people in his community. She personally doesn't enjoy being in a sauna, her body is often already on fire, without any additional heat! Nevertheless, she can enjoy the enjoyments of others.

To share skills with each other is such a treasure.

With every exploration she gets a little closer to herself, accepting herself a bit more. With every step she takes towards appreciating others and herself, inner peace follows.

QUESTIONS

- Are you open to getting sweaty and even dirty?
- Do you like to use your bare hands or be barefooted?
- When do you feel totally alive using your hands?
- Do you like to evolve your senses? Which ones?
- What about the sensation of the touch with your hands and with your fingertips? A haptic exploration.
- Are you interested in different kinds of creations and handcrafts other than the digital world?
- What would you love to create just for fun?

Lifehack: Get some ideas, material, an easy introduction, and just go for it.

Taking portraits of models or people who are used to being in front of a camera is an entirely different experience compared to exposing yourself as an amateur behind the lens. Can you imagine how vulnerable this may feel?

INTERACTION WITH THE CAMERA
PART 1 – STUNNING PORTRAITS

She is so happy to be a participant in a practical workshop on how to create showstopping portraits with her own camera. It's all about the different settings, the aperture, the shutter, the IOS, and how to have the correct focus on the light. The composition and the expression are vitally significant too. Having the opportunity to have a female and a male model, who are both used to be in front of the camera, is a bonus. For her it's challenging to look at someone who stares back at her in such a confident direct way, while waiting patiently to move into certain positions. She even kneels on the floor to get the perfect shot. The results are stunning, especially when she allows herself to be a part of the connection between the model and the camera. It's like a dance, a sensual, playful, but serious interaction. The space is safe enough to bring the best out of the person who is in front of her and the camera and allows them to identify their freedom of privilege to express their personality and emotions. Laughter is one of the tools she uses to surprise the well-experienced models and to create a more personalized approach. The wonder and mystery of their rawness is highlighted. She loves to support and advance the development of the people who get in contact with her. After she has taken the photos of the models, she is left blushing. She is not used to flirting with someone, especially not in such an obvious way. Now it's her turn to step into the role of the model. She knows it will be both a huge challenge and a real gain for her personal growth. She feels her heartbeat rapidly increasing after making the decision to accept the challenge. Even though it's only in front of her classmates, it's odd, unfamiliar, and uncomfortable for her. She doesn't know how to pose, where to put her arms, or where to look. It's such a different experience for her compared to being behind the camera, to being the one who focuses on the model, to suddenly being the one who is being looked at, not only by one person, but the whole group. A new world is revealed to her. Being stared at by her classmates who stand very close to her, using their telephoto lenses to take some shots, is almost crippling. Her mind is busy, running wild. If she is not careful, the monkey mind will jump in and tell her she isn't a real contribution to the group, or that she isn't photogenic or attractive enough. Such nonsense, but still with such power over her. No child is born to think about whether they are pretty enough or doubting whether they are good or perfect enough to fit in with society. What happens between the years of being a small child and growing up to be an adult? Judgement and comparison sneak in and make themselves comfortable all while being enforced by caregivers and school systems. It's not done intentionally but more so by unfulfilled self-worth. Self-love and self-esteem are so vital for us to thrive, and must be consciously invited in. This experience gives her a vibrant glow, and she shines proudly, knowing she is enough. More than enough.

QUESTIONS

- With whom do you feel most comfortable?
- With whom do you share a safe space to experience yourself in an unrestricted way?
- Where are you right now with your confidence?
- Are there situations where you feel comfortable being exposed, being noticed?
- How strong is your self-esteem and self-respect?
- What about judgement and comparison? Do they have power in your life?
- With whom do you compare yourself?
- Do you catch yourself judging yourself even more than others do?
- What is self-love to you?
- How do you practice self-love daily?

Imagine you get asked to be a part of a video, a short sequence in which you express your gratitude. Would you be open to showing yourself in a vulnerable way? Sometimes even one word can carry a message and touch people's hearts.

INTERACTION WITH THE CAMERA
PART 2 – THE THANK YOU VIDEO

She decides she wants to experience the process of creating a video from beginning to end. To generate something wonderful which touches the hearts of many people. First there is the idea to interview different people, with different backgrounds, ages, genders, and cultures. It becomes evident that two short words, *Thank you*, should be used. The reference point is to think about and picture a person, or several people, they are thankful for. It can be a pet, a personal experience, or a situation in their life for which they feel gratitude.

She buys an optimal microphone, a camera and a tripod to fix it on.

She writes on a piece of paper all the names of the people who she can think of who would be interested in taking part in the video. She is quite extroverted, but she finds it difficult to ask people for this favor. On the other hand, she is more than open to supporting her friends.

It's all about being ready to face possible rejection and not taking it personally. Some people are shy and don't like to expose themselves to an unknown audience. Some people want to stay in control. She likes to connect with the people in the video before and during the filming. This helps to build trust and a safe space for people to be authentic. To be that close to the person, with his or her feelings and their personal expression of gratitude, is such an intimate moment. It's like connecting to a higher power.

The locations for filming are either out in nature, in the Alps, in a city park, garden or at a lake. Somewhere where the participants will feel at home, or at the very least, comfortable. Some shoots are planned with friends of hers and others are spontaneous encounters. What rich diversity, connecting with people's souls, having the opportunity to give something back, a moment of mindfulness and awareness of the present and all its opportunities. A teenage girl wants to be a part of the video even though she is still learning how to be comfortable in her own skin. Others join in- an entire family, seniors, playful grown-up men with boyhood in their eyes, vulnerability shown by conscious men, a woman who tears up while saying thank you through the lens of the camera – all such sacred moments to witness. The gift of their gratitude touches her heart so intensely, it opens her up even more for loving and being of service to people. An important reason for why she creates this video is to take the time to connect with every participant while looking through all the video material she has taken upon completion of the project. It is work and passion at the same time. She must have the end result in mind, visually and emotionally, while cutting and arranging the clips to create a full video, with flow and music in the background. It's like sprinkling powdered sugar on a piece of soul cake. It's so sweet and satisfying. Gratitude is contagious and can be spread to all the different parts of the world.

QUESTIONS

- What would you like to create or invent that touches the hearts of even just one human being?
- Have you found a way to connect with your higher power/ higher source/ higher self?
- Who or what is your higher power?
- How do you see yourself being of service to others?
- What is your life's mission?
- Who or what would you like to get in contact with to let them know how grateful you are for who they are in your life and in this world?
- What could you be more grateful for? Write it down.
- What would you love to give yourself more appreciation for?
- Why not give yourself a "Thank you" whenever you look into a mirror?

Lifehack: Create a gratitude journal if you don't already have one. Write down five things you are grateful for daily. You could expand it by not only writing words and sentences, but by sketching something too if you feel like it. Don't overthink it- have fun and get creative!

Are you comfortable enough to share your story in front of a group of people, maybe even strangers? Revealing yourself in different facets, not holding back. Sharing what you have accomplished, as well your struggles and how you overcame them. Knowing that your story can be a contribution to someone's life, giving them hope, helping them not to feel broken or alone, that there is a solution for anything we are faced with. This is how hope is created. You are welcome to see how she prepares herself for it.

TELL YOUR STORY

She is invited to speak at an event which is called: *Tell your story*. She prepares for it by diving deep into her story. Suddenly, doubts and uncertainty come up. Who doesn't know this self-destructive monkey mind all too well, always whispering in your ear and belittling you, trying to persuade you to pull out of any situation that is new or challenging, luring you not to take the risk or the chance to shine? Questions come up like: Is her story important enough to be told? Would anyone even be interested in hearing it at all? She hasn't experienced violence, abuse, poverty, or drugs. But she is aware that she must still process certain things in her life, past and present.

Every life has its own rules and perceptions of what makes a personal story worth telling.

Who gets to decide what is significant and what's not? Everyone has experienced challenges in their lives, either in their childhood, as a teenager, or as an adult. Every life has its own high and lows.

She knows and is certain that no one can live someone else's life, no matter how hard they try. Therefore, everyone must learn to help themselves, and if needed, ask for help and support from a professional. Not holding onto drama and rising above it, creating something good and powerful out of it, is the key to lasting peace and joy. That's a gamechanger.

To get out of the victim mentality into a self-improved life has always been her goal.

She realizes while she goes through the stages of her life and puts down on paper those lessons which life taught her, that the word *sorry* has always been her companion. She struggled with low self-worth and making excuses for nearly everything. "Sorry" was a first name and family name for her for decades.

She decides to share this during her speech. She also shares her experience with anxiety and claustrophobia and how she got through it and transformed it into an opportunity to grow and learn something new about herself. Whenever a "sorry" shows up that's ok, too. To not fight against it is so freeing. She also includes the question: *How to find the balance between being significant and insignificant?*

Another insight of hers is how having empathy towards others and their stories as well as taking good care of herself is the key to her happiness.

Now it's clear to her that people will hear about her struggles and how she overcomes them. How she improves her self-esteem and self-love to the point where she feels stronger, more courageous in areas where she once believed she was weak.

It's important for her to share and encourage her audience not to hold onto the past, but instead focus on where they would like to go, what they would like to experience in their lives. What they dream of. She encourages them to be proud of what they have already achieved, and how they can allow happiness to be a part of their lives no matter what.

She will take some pictures to the event, pictures showing her challenging situations, and she knows she will be a good contribution to the event, bringing inspiration and hope to others.

Just being her, vulnerable and real. She feels so privileged to have been considered. What joy and gratitude she has for this opportunity.

Living the greatest version of her life possible. From a maybe, to a yes.

QUESTIONS

- Are you aware that your story can be a contribution to someone else's life?
- Which situations come to mind?
- Are you a good listener too?
- How do you cope with your monkey mind? Can you engage with your monkey to make sure that it doesn't prevent you from taking risks?
- What words do you use that aren't serving you anymore?
- Where do you still live in the past, and do you realize it's not a helpful contribution to your future?
- How would you like to experience yourself in the upcoming years?
- What legacy would you love to leave behind, when it's time to say goodbye to this life?

Lifehack: You are the creator of your life. Every day you get a new chance to be the greatest version of you, without force and judgment, but with ease and joy.

A real adventure for her, and maybe not for other people, is daily life once in a while. To be out in rough nature is still mystical to her. She needs certain things to make sure that she feels comfortable and confident in her daily life. She has some tools and a first-aid tool kit, which she has access to. Are you able to be adaptable enough that you can make yourself feel safe in unusual situations?

YURT PART 1

She has this wonderful idea to surprise her husband with a stay in a Yurt for his birthday. She realizes that she must arrange and organize herself very well in advance.

It's wintertime and freezing cold. They get to the parking lot at the bottom of the mountain. They are so lucky and more than happy that they don't have to carry everything up to the top of the mountain, because they can use the snow mobile. With a swing and some muscle power, they are able to place their backpacks with all their belongings on the special baggage tray at the back of the snow mobile. They have to sit very close to the driver, but they don't mind at all. As long as they don't have to hike up the hill in the stormy and foggy weather, they are happy. They could even get lost in this unpleasant deep winter. The ride takes approximately twenty minutes. They hold tightly to the snowmobile, making sure not to fall off and hurt themselves. They are soon relieved that the bumpy road trip is over. She takes a deep breath as they arrive at the plateau of the Alps.

Five white Yurts welcome them like monuments. There is a main wooden building with a kitchen, dining guest room, and a small wooden building for the shower/ bathroom. Everything is nestled against the white snowy mountains, and it looks like a fairytale.

She could sense the adventure right from the beginning. Not knowing how she will cope being up here in the wild of nature, with only a tent to separate her from the elements, is refreshing. When she made the reservation, the owner of the Yurts mentioned on the phone that she doesn't have to worry about the sub-zero temperatures. Every Yurt has an electric heater. Her first instinct was to take a sleeping bag with her, but after the phone call, she decided to leave it at home. She always prefers to be prepared and to not rely on anyone else, just in case.

Here it comes, get ready to see your personal Yurt! There is a king-size bed with two duvets, and in the middle of the room is a wood-heated oven and an electric heater on the side. But it doesn't work. It broke down one day before they arrived. Right now, it's just there for decoration. This could be quite a tough adventure knowing that she won't be able to just walk down to the bottom of the mountain if claustrophobia or anxiety take over. It's very dangerous to be outside and further way from the Yurts in the night, because with the fog and the large amounts of snow, and the ongoing snowfall, you could get lost.

She hears herself saying, *Just relax, you will survive. There are only so many hours until the morning comes, so just breathe and stay in the present.*

She knows herself well enough. To feel safe, she has to get everything which she really needs in place, like a torch and some rescue drops, and she has to give herself the freedom to stay up even if it means being awake through the night. If she needs to get totally dressed up in her protective winter ski clothes with cap and gloves to go out and walk through the deep snow to the main building to find a mug to have some water in her Yurt, she will do it. She doesn't shame herself for having some rituals which help her cope in uncertain and unfamiliar situations. Especially knowing that the claustrophobia or anxiety could suddenly occur out of nowhere.

Yes, drinking some water always helps to calm her down and decreases her stress levels.

Knowing that there is a separate bathroom building with a working heating system on the wall gives her more confidence. The option to stay there if the Yurt is too cold calms her, as she knows she can stay there if she becomes uncomfortable during the night. She can sit next to the toilet and the warm cozy heating system and not care what others will say or think of her.

She makes the choice to take responsibility for herself despite it being an adventure trip. She loves to feel comfortable.

QUESTIONS

- How do you soothe yourself if stress or fear occur?
- What are some rituals which help you to cope in uncertain and unfamiliar situations?
- Do you still care about what others will say or think of you?
- Where would you like to take more responsibility for, and to take better care of, yourself?

Lifehack: If you are in a stressful situation, even with anxiety, say to yourself: This won't last forever! Extraordinary situations demand exceptional actions.

Do you like to serve your loved ones? To take care of them in original ways? She finds herself in quite an adventurous setting, celebrating her hubby's birthday. Why not treat him like a king? She has to get organized and do whatever it takes to make this an adventure of love.

YURT PART 2

They must use a wooden basket to get the wood for the fireplace into the Yurt. It is already cut into small pieces and is waiting in a special hut close to the main building to be used. Their Yurt is furthest from the main building. This requires a lot of energy, especially in temperatures around 20° below Celsius. It's so cold inside the Yurt that they can see small clouds in the air coming out of their mouths with every breath. It's as if they are smoking. The freezing cold evening and night offers a sky filled with bright shining stars. It's so amazing to look at. They are wrapped in blankets, lying in a real bed to stay as warm as possible. She would like to treat her hubby like a birthday king, so she gets up whenever needed, to make sure the fire doesn't extinguish. She enjoys putting another pile of wood into the oven until the stove pipe is nearly glowing. A lot of heat is created this way, but it is not long-lasting. She uses her iPhone as an alarm clock to remind her to add new wood at certain times, but she doesn't consider that wearing the monkey cap to keep warm will prevent her from hearing the alarm clock going off. When she is woken up by the cold of her cheeks and nose which are exposed to the air, she realizes she didn't hear the alarm clock and the fire went out. The candle in the Yurt still provides some light. She feels like a scout on an important mission, in this case: her and her hubby's wellbeing. She quickly jumps into her clothes and her winter boots and puts thick gloves on to open the metal oven which is dangerously hot. She feels the energy of adventure in her veins. Relying on her creativity, she uses a wooden stick to ensure she does not touch the door and burn herself while opening it to add more wood. Happily, she looks at her husband who is still sleeping, only his nose sticking out from under the duvet. She wants to keep them nice and warm. But the cozy heat disappears so quickly, out through the chimney. Outside of the Yurt, sparks of embers are floating up into the cold freezing air towards the sky. As long as she is preoccupied doing something, she feels more comfortable. She also feels like making a contribution to herself and her hubby. She jumps into bed again and is more than happy and satisfied. When she steps out of the Yurt into the silence of nature the next morning, an extraordinary blue sky with the electrifyingly bright, clean new white snow and impressive cold air welcomes her. She is so proud that she took the chance to step out of her comfort zone to have such an amazing experience for herself and her hubby. It is immensely comforting knowing she can rely on herself if she needs to. After having a rich breakfast, they get a sledge to ride down the hill. Laughter follows them, and they are filled with gratitude and joy to have experienced such a wonderful time, far away from any population, noises and pollution. She is in charge of her own happiness. What a positive outcome: to overcome her own fears and get in touch with an ancient part of herself. Her trust in life and her own power within warms her.

QUESTIONS

- How important is your birthday to you?
- Do you like to be treated as a birthday queen or king?
- Where and when do you still fall off the wagon and blame someone else for your life and your decisions, or your unhappiness?
- What situation pops up where you deeply trusted life and experienced your own power at the same time?
- Where would you like to say goodbye to victimhood and instead own it and step into your immense power?

Lifehack: YES, you are accountable for and in charge of your own happiness!

What comes to mind when you think of surfing? Is it to be wild, free, independent, in alignment with the elements, especially with the water and the waves? Is it about the actual sport or is it linked to a certain lifestyle, community, being relaxed, waiting for the waves, or letting loose? Join her at her first surf camp and find out for yourself.

SURF CAMP PART 1

She hums the song *Surfin' USA*. No, she isn't heading to the USA but her and her hubby are going to Portugal to surf. It's a great location, and no, it won't be the spot for the world's most advanced surfers, but for beginners like her! Fifty-five years old, learning how to surf, and imagining herself as a surfer girl, gives her a spark of pleasure and a giggle. Her cells are all activated just thinking about this special vacation. She doesn't really know why she is constantly challenging herself. This time she and her hubby will not stay in a comfortable hotel; instead, she decided to book a glamping experience, a mixture of camping and glamour. They will be situated at a camping site, a private area with the glamping tents and the surfing community.

When they arrive, it's obvious that the two of them are the oldest ones in the whole surf camp. Most of them could be their daughters or sons. It's easy to notice who the surfing instructors among the other people are. They either have blonde hair, are kissed from the sun and washed out from the salty seawater, or are intensely suntanned. The cliché is true, all the teachers have a sexy surfer-body. That's not quite the situation with her body, but hey, what other options does she have right now? Having chosen to try surfing only few weeks before means that no intense workouts or weight loss programs were going to create a twenty-year-old surfer girl! She can choose to use what she has and where she is physically, or she can wait for the right moment and risk that there will never be a right moment. Rather go with the flow and live in the now. They get to see their glamping tent. What a dream! The tent is made of beige-colored outdoor canvas fabric, and inside is a double bed, a small side table, two bed lamps, a green plant, and a chair. There's a small patio with two wooden chairs and a wooden table that belongs to their tent. It looks like the same one which she saw in a magazine that she got the idea from. The view is spectacular. The tents are located right on the top of the cliffs, where the infinite blue ocean can be seen below them. The restaurant is a nicely decorated outdoor open tent with a canvas roof and some bamboo pillars. The food gets freshly prepared and cooked in front of the guests, and it's a feast to eat. Easy and relaxed. The whole area is surrounded by sand, and it's lovely to walk barefoot. It's still a good idea to keep an eye on the sharp pine needles!

The staff are welcoming and relaxed. There is music in the background and the surf boards are stored by color like a rainbow.

They all get an introduction to and about the equipment, wetsuits, boards, the rules, the weekly activity plan, and the campus.

They will have lessons according to the daily tides, and this could be in the late afternoon, or very early in the morning. To learn to surf requires a lot of muscle power and endurance. First, they must carry the longboard, which is optimal for beginners, down the narrow sandy path to the beach. She wears her wetsuit halfway to her hips, ready to pull up the top half later, after the warmup is done. The waves come in and out. She, her hubby and all the other students must lie with their bellies on their boards in the sand to practice the technique of standing up. There are different ways to get up, and it depends on muscle power, speed, strength, agility and balance. Her hubby is like a young surfer, he is quickly able to pop up and surf his first small waves. What a great surprise. Not everyone has such luck right at the beginning. She has some difficulty with her left hip, she never noticed this handicap before. Up until now, nothing in her life has ever restricted her. She struggles to get standing up on the board because she is unable to make the move which is needed. She has tears in her eyes; it can be frustrating not to get this. Still, even as a good swimmer, it's a new experience for her to learn to get comfortable with. She runs into the waves of the white water, splashing directly into her face, then diving underneath a wave which comes towards her, turning the board in the right direction, then jumping on it. It's a lot to take on. While lying on the board with her belly, waiting until the right wave comes, she hears the surf teacher shouting: *Paddle, paddle, paddle, go!* She tries to balance and get up, only to lose her balance and find herself in the water again. This goes on for some time. She feels like she is training with the navy seals. She is as exhausted as one! To have the ability and empathy to cheer others up, to applaud them, to celebrate them and enjoy their success with them is activating her inner willpower and stamina. After five days of trying over and over again, having recovered from criticizing herself for not getting up, enjoying the sea, being physical and getting to be a part of the ocean, it happens. It's the big final; she has her last run, her lovely and patient surf instructor from Australia says to her: *Listen, "this" will be your last wave and you will get up, get into the surf position and ride her.* Her body and mind are totally alerted. She can feel it, now it's her turn, her run. The wave is coming from behind towards the tail of her board, and he shouts, *Paddle, paddle, paddle, go!* She gathers all her energy and stands up for the FIRST time and surfs towards the beach! What an inexpressible feeling. Everyone in the water and at the beach is rejoicing. She weeps with relief and gratitude when she gets out of the water. Her hubby receives her with tears of joy in his eyes, and she falls into his arms. Their surf instructor gets out of the water too, to hug and congratulate her. Everywhere she looks around, surfers make the special surfer hand sign to her... YES, you've done it.

QUESTIONS

- Do you remember situations when you told yourself: it's not the right time, you're not the right shape, not the right age?
- What would you do differently now?
- Are you good at making decisions?
- Are you ready to unlearn your procrastinating habits? What are they?
- Are you good at finding excuses?
- How do you cope with frustration or failure? What are your solutions?
- What about empathy, does it come easily to you?
- Are you able to cheer others up, celebrate their success with them, or do you have envy because you want to be in their place and situation?
- What activates your inner willpower and stamina?

Lifehack: Imagine yourself being where you would like to be. Use your senses to see and feel yourself as if you are already there and have already achieved what is important for you.

After getting to know the camp, the crew and the surfing spot, she feels a connection. Appreciating others is a gift. Why don't you loosen up your tired leg muscles and move? Try a surf camp. Surprise yourself!

SURF CAMP PART 2

Everyone gets together because the crew has to make an announcement. It's an award ceremony. Her name is called out, and she is awarded for having the most endurance and never giving up. This is because she had the capacity to focus on her development and progression, as well as see it in others and even communicating it to them. Everyone applauds her while she goes up to the mic and takes in the appreciation with gratitude. She knows how to share her own joy and to receive and delight in the joy of others. Choosing to be vulnerable is a gift for others and inspires them to open up too. She is suddenly a role model for others, even the younger generations. Age isn't important. Who you are inside is what counts.

She is curious to see how the staff lives out here and heads towards the crew camp. She notices that there are items of clothing hanging everywhere. Ropes which are fixed from one pine tree to another, or from tent to tent, hold all their personal wetsuits, swimming trunks and bikinis. Aloha! The atmosphere is very laid-back and welcoming. When they see her curiosity for their world, they proudly invite her to view the interior of their tents. The volunteers have to share tents. Their tent has a middle part, some space to sit down, and two girls even have a small carpet on the floor to sit on. Theme: How to make your small world cozy and practical. The instructors who stay there for the duration of the season have a tent of their own. She is invited to those tents too. One of the male surfers even has hangers in his tent to put his colored shirts on. Her surf instructor has his surfboard and bodyboard in his tent. This place is a nice breather for the staff when they want to spend some time away from the guests and have some time on their own. They appreciate that she is so interested in their lives. Their main life is either at the beach, in the ocean, on the board, or at the main camp where they prepare activities.

It's a privilege to have a look into and explore an unfamiliar world, without having to live there.

Besides the surf lessons, yoga and some other activities are offered during the daytime and evenings too. In the bar area, there is a balance board and a ramp for skaters waiting to be used. She is receptive, and her world expands with each passing day. When she and her hubby get invited to attend a dance competition in the evening, she assesses whether or not they have enough energy to make it. They feel worn out after a full day of activities and surfing. The instructors persuade them to join for this event. She already feels her fatigued muscles hurting. When they arrive at the sandy meeting point, everything is already organized. With a rope and some wooden pegs, a square is created, spotlights are installed, and there's a table for the judges. DJ equipment is set outside the boxing ring. Everyone is excited. She and her hubby haven't been dancing for quite some time. The DJ plays some music to warm up the participants who are waiting to hear the rules. First rule: Every couple must move and dance at all times, even when the music stops. Second rule: Always smile at each other. Third rule: Always have eye contact with your partner, even when turning around or changing position. Before they start, she and her hubby agree to give it a try, even if they get kicked out after five or ten minutes. Expectations are often flawed. This often happens to the two of them. After being cheered on by the competitors who were already asked to leave the "boxing ring", she and her hubby danced in the sand for two full hours. With this, first place was inevitable.

For them it's such a huge learning curve, dancing and winning. In all the years before, they've never had as much continuous eye contact with each other. What a gift to their marriage.

It was always her dream to find herself in a place where kindness, openness, humor and expression have meaning and significance. Her heart is overflowing. What an epic community to be a part of.

QUESTIONS

- Where and with whom do you enjoy delighting in the joy of others?
- Are you able to get vulnerable before others to inspire others to follow?
- How do you inspire others?
- Where and to whom are you a role model without trying to be one?
- Are you a role model for younger generations?
- What do you think about your age?
- Where do you use your age as an excuse for not trying?
- Have you ever experienced the magic of continuous eye contact with a loved one?
- What is something you like to experience with your partner that would deepen your connection as a couple?
- Where does your soul feel totally at home? More than one option is possible.
- What qualities do you find there?

Have you ever written a book, or do you dream of writing a book? It's a journey, a quest to find your unique voice, connecting with your true feelings, and struggling with self-doubt. It's about facing procrastination, asking yourself if there are people longing to read this kind of content and if they will love your way of expressing yourself? There will be a moment when it's crystal clear that it doesn't matter whether you touch a lot of people with your writing or your insights, that one will be enough. If one reader gets stimulated, inspired, finds hope, or a way back to their own power, or even explores their genius for the first time, it is still worth it.

WRITING THE FIRST BOOK

What has inspired her to even think of writing a book? In her case it hasn't been her dream from childhood, and it certainly didn't come up as a desire in her early adulthood. She never quite saw writing as a skill of hers. Being told as a child that she has to practice writing because hers was unreadable and that she wasn't allowed to have her own personalized handwriting didn't inspire her at all. She never got praise for her own unique way of expressing herself through written words. She never got credit for what she liked to share on a birthday card or in a letter; it was never good enough. So, she lost interest in writing. Journaling is still an option to her. To be able to write in a safe space free from criticism is appealing. She remembers holding the book of a 20-year-old writer in her hand, reading the foreword of the author: "Don't worry about the spelling, the right grammar, I'm not worried either. Instead, just read the book from your heart and if you do so, you'll get the real message and meaning behind the words."

It took her years to get the confidence that this young woman had already developed at such an early age. Everyone has a history, a story to tell- when they felt shame, blamed and not good enough. It doesn't matter if the validation you sought was through writing, presenting, singing, acting, drawing, painting, playing an instrument, dancing, crafting, creating. If validation didn't matter, what would you allow your inner child to experience? Would you encourage your younger self to explore life to the fullest? Be wild, unstoppable and proud of yourself. That's what the author of this book, the one you are holding right now, is pointing out. Her approach in writing this book is to reveal stories of where she came from. Sharing openly what her challenges were, even if no one in the world can relate. The main goal of writing this book is to give hope, show others how to overcome obstacles, inspire others to follow their dreams. Living with vulnerability but power.

We are human beings with infinite possibilities, skills, and capacities, and are as colorful and versatile as the galaxies. Looking at the ways we cope with fear, anxiety, depression, self-doubt, feelings of not being good enough and transforming these into joy, fulfillment, self-love, and purpose is one of the biggest challenges for us wonderful human beings. It doesn't matter what your age is, what your gender is, where you come from, and what the color of your skin is. It's all about the true connection with the powerful and shining soul inside you, with all the creativity, energy, consciousness, and heart quality. The part of you that wants to be expressed in a raw and uncensored way. Leaving all concepts of right and wrong and comparisons behind, you will find that you are more than capable of doing anything you set your mind to. She did.

QUESTIONS

- What did you never get praise for, but still long for?
- Could it be genius to perform in your unique way?
- What would you like to share with the world? Writing, dancing, singing, acting?
- What is your calling, where do you feel yourself drawn to?
- What is your real power, your uniqueness?
- What are your standards?
- Have you already created a dream list, your heart list?
- Which dreams of yours are desperately waiting to be lived out by you right now?

Lifehack: No one can do you better than you do! You are good enough, so be wild and free, unstoppable, and proud of yourself!

These QR codes will open the doors
to a wonderous universe for you.
A Shower Inspiration Meditation

The Shower Inspiration Meditation is a short, easy-to-use free meditation perfect for while taking a relaxing shower or sitting comfortably somewhere quiet, to enthuse you to find out more about your deepest dreams and desires and encourage you to put them on your heart list and explore them. SHINE!

My Facebook Group

My Facebook group is a sacred space for you to share the successes of your own Sonja Moments, your SHINE Moments; to share the challenges you have overcome and to connect with others who are also on their heart journeys. The group is for encouraging one another and is a way for you to find out about my offers and programs- and occasionally have a Zoom session to get to know your SHINE! community.

If you are reflecting on your life and asking yourself, is this all? And you would like to work with me on your SHINE! transformation, just visit www.sonja-shine.com.

Never forget you are WONDERFUL and more than ENOUGH.

www.ingramcontent.com/pod-product-compliance
Lightning Source LLC
Chambersburg PA
CBHW051425290426
44109CB00016B/1437